Cuban Stories

Cuban Stories

about

People, Terraces, Food, Revolution, and Good-bye's

by

María Martínez Aenlle

ISBN 978-0-557-98695-8

ACKNOWLEDGMENTS

I thank my mother, Marietta Aenlle y de Vega, and my sister, América Isabel Martínez Aenlle, for encouraging me to write my memories. I was able to check family and historical facts with my mother, who never forgets anything and is our family historian. She also helped me to edit the Spanish version of this book. Whenever I had doubts about writing, my sister provided spiritual support for me to keep going to tell my stories. She became my book editor, too. I thank my father, Juan Antonio Martínez González, who passed away before I wrote this book of stories, for always providing me insights into our Cuban history and political past.

CONTENTS

INTRODUCTION

This book is a collection of memories from my childhood in Cuba. Most memories are about my family life a few years before the Cuban Revolution. I also remember the first two years of the Revolution, a time of upheaval until the country became communist. My memories became stories about the things I loved about Cuba, the customs of my family, and the sudden changes in our lives. Life changed overnight, and it has never been the same.

Cuba continues to be in the news, a subject of interest to many Americans. Through these stories, I share the magic of pre-revolutionary Cuba, a place that will not be known to future visitors of the Island, or to new Cuban generations because those times are now gone. My memories are always with me and they focus on the following stories:

- The Things I Loved Most about Cuba
- Cuba's Terraces, Patios, and Courtyards
- Vacationing in Cuban Beaches and Countryside
- Cuba Starts to Change
- In the U.S.A.

I invite you to take a trip down my Cuban memory lane.

ONE

LIFE IN EL VEDADO

I enjoyed living in El Vedado with its beautiful streets, houses and mansions, movie theatres, and restaurants. The neighborhood of El Vedado, the oldest suburb of Havana, became another section of the city and also home to the Cemetery of Colón. I enjoyed life's little routines in my neighborhood, taking them for granted without knowing how much they would mean to me later when they were gone.

My week was full of school activities, but I always made time to go for afternoon walks with my grandmother and to watch TV in the evening while doing my homework. Weekends were the time to go out with my parents. Saturdays meant going to the Trianón or Payret movie houses or to El Cinecito, a theatre for kids. We saw American films with Spanish subtitles, such as *April Love*, *The Red Shoes*, or cowboy and Indian pictures, and, sometimes, French films. Spanish films were also popular, especially if Sarita Montiel, a young and pretty singer and actress from Spain, starred in them. I remember watching *And God Created Woman*, starring Brigitte Bardot, better known as BB. The film made headlines because the new French actress appeared partially nude on the screen. My parents and I liked the film. It was not X-rated, although my parents later thought it should have been. I thought BB was pretty with a good figure, and I thought she had courage for doing such a risqué film. We watched *Room at the Top*, another new release starring Simone Signoret and Lawrence Harvey. When the film ended, I overheard my parents saying, "This should have been rated differently; we should not have brought her," meaning me. I was glad that I saw the film, for it touched me and made me think. Actually, I liked it quite a bit. I was totally absorbed by the film's story of love, betrayal, and torment where the wrong person was loved for the wrong motives, ending in suicide and remorse. Well, I was convinced children always knew and understood more than their parents would like to think.

My favorite movie house was El Cinecito. I always looked forward to intermission time. The only lights in the dark theatre were those of the cartoons of Tom & Jerry, Mickey Mouse, and Betty Boop. Then, all of a sudden, it was time for the toy raffle to start, the moment all kids anticipated. My heart raced rapidly while I waited to see if I would win a prize. I usually won something, but when my number was called, I was too shy to go down to pick it up by myself. My father accompanied me to say thank you and collect the prize while all eyes stared at us. After the raffle, we watched the black-and-white news reel. The reel had an upsetting impact on me in the midst of funny cartoons and coming attractions. I liked the funnies because they were in color, but much to my disappointment, sometimes they showed an older one in black and white. I was convinced that a malfunctioning bulb behind the screen was to be blamed for the lack of colors. After the movies, we went to eat pancakes, or flying saucer sandwiches. The sandwiches were made with ham, Swiss cheese, and white bread slices pressed into a round, flat shape to look like a flying saucer out of a Flash Gordon episode. I ate the hot sandwich accompanied by a thick and frosty chocolate shake.

Sunday was a busy day for us. My dad and I went early to the market to shop for fresh fish and meat for our week's meals. Our last stop was the bakery where we got our crusty Cuban bread. We went to Mass at El Carmelo, the church near our home, in the afternoon. We nicknamed the church El Derrumbe, meaning The Tumbling Down because of its dilapidated look. I liked going to that church and hearing Mass in Latin. I could hardly understand Latin, but its sound made me feel closer to heaven. The church was across the park where I played with my dad and rode my bike. I wondered how many more years the church would withstand the rain and sun beating on it before it actually tumbled down, hopefully at a moment when it was empty. Finally, the priests built a modern building in the shape of a V and annexed it to the old church. We were all relieved.

After Mass we went to Havana's Cemetery of Colón to visit my grandmother's grave. The cemetery was large and beautiful with what I later learned were Egyptian and Italian influences. According to my parents, its design made it stand amongst the world's famous cemeteries, such as La Recoleta in Buenos Aires and Pere Lachaisse in Paris. Family tombs varied in size and design.

White, gray, and rose marble were the preferred colors for the private pantheons where family members were buried. Statues of angels, saints, and the Virgin Mary presided over the tombs as if guarding them. A Galician architect by the name of Calixto Arellano de Loira y Cardoso designed the cemetery. My great grandfather, José de Vega Flores, also a Spanish architect and structural engineer, designed and built its main entrance gate. Mother always made sure that I knew our family's history, and in this case, it made me proud. We went by bus to the cemetery, my father's preferred way of getting around based on the populist side of his personality. Once there, I never remembered how to get to our family's tomb, an early sign that I was to have a bad sense of direction. The visit to the grave of my deceased grandmother was important for my mother. Father and I understood it well. I had felt great love for my maternal grandmother and missed her. She left a big void in our lives for many years after her death. Praying and placing flowers on her tombstone on a quiet and peaceful afternoon made us feel that she was still among us, and she was.

Lunch followed at a small restaurant on 23rd Street, a boulevard of El Vedado, busy with pedestrians visiting shops, restaurants, and theatres. We had two favorite restaurants, a Chinese place, which later became a favorite of Fidel Castro, and the Restaurant of 23rd street, where we ate *fritas*, the Cuban version of a hamburger. The small fried hamburgers were topped with shoestring potatoes, whose crushing noise made them even better.

Other days took us to El Carmen, a Spanish bodega whose outdoor restaurant was covered with a green valance. El Carmen was located at the corners of 15th and 23rd Streets in El Vedado, close to our flat on 20th Street. They served light snacks, typical of Cuba and Spain. We usually ordered café au lait with warm buttered toast. Comfortable brown chairs and tables were found on a terrace that surrounded the bodega. We enjoyed the breeze and watched people and neighbors go by as we sat under the green cloth valance. Before leaving, my father went to the bodega's counter to buy Spanish hams and cheeses or rice and beans by the pound to take home. I followed him to the bodega to listen to the heavy Castilian accent of the owner. I stood there peeking behind the counter whose floors were covered with sawdust to prevent the attendants from slipping. Those Spaniards were efficient and attentive but somewhat distant. Their typical austere and stoic attitude was part of our own character. That is how my father was. He and my mother were both descendants of Spanish Celts from Galicia.

Mother and I regularly visited the Woolworth's store, a popular thing to do. We referred to the store as Tencen, leaving out the "ts" at the end of the word, as was usual in our Cuban pronunciation. The first Tencen was located at the corners of San Rafael and Indusria. In the 1930s, a larger Tencen replaced it at the corner of Galiano and San Rafael streets in Havana. It stood across from El Encanto, a legendary and stylish department store. Later, another Tencen opened in El Vedado, which was conveniently located for us. The waitresses served sandwiches and banana splits to those seated at the counter while other customers waited their turn to grab a place to sit. The store had a permanent bustle from people looking for bargains, snacking at the counter, or just having a good time. Our favorite snack was the Special sandwich, a hamburger bun filled with a spread made of mayonnaise, ham, and pickles. The Special came wrapped in an opaque baking parchment paper, something I thought was different. We always drank a Coca-Cola with our Special sandwich. Everyone we knew visited the Tencen to shop for bargains and novelties from the United States. Mother still has a black Bakelite ring with a pearl that my father bought for her at the store. She lost the fake pearl, and loved the ring so much, that she replaced it with a cultured pearl. She still receives compliments on her Tencen ring, by now an antique. Who would have known?

Sometimes we stopped by El Encanto to see the latest but expensive merchandise. El Encanto was a visual treat, with its beautiful automated escalators, on which I jumped right away, and its creative decorations and mirrors, similar to what I later would see at a Saks Fifth Avenue or Lord and Taylor store in the United States. El Encanto's female employees did not wear uniforms but were always dressed in white during the summer and in black during winter to match the seasons. Unfortunately, El Encanto disappeared, burned to the ground by a bomb explosion. Years later, the store was rebuilt, but was never the same as before.

After seeing a movie, we went to La Rampa section in El Vedado to have ice cream. The section had theatres, TV and radio stations, the latest boutiques, and the best ice cream shop in the city. Our favorite ice cream flavor was anon, made out of the tropical fruit. The anon fruit is about the size of an orange with light green and thick skin in the shape of scales. Each scale has fruit pulp and a black seed. Its texture is creamy, the flavor sweet, floral, and delicate. We ate our ice cream out of a paper cup with a little wooden spoon. We enjoyed the ice cream under a starry night, feeling the sea breeze from Havana's bay.

Even after the Revolution took over the government and our lives, we still went to see an American movie, as a small act of defiance, and to get ice cream. We kept our routine and asked what flavors the shop had. The attendant looked at us seriously and said, "Vanilla, vanilla, and vanilla. You want vanilla, right?" Laughingly we answered, "Sure, vanilla, our favorite." "Good choice. It's coming up," the attendant said. There was a twinkle in his eyes, showing the typical Cuban sense of humor that came in handy when dealing with adversity.

Father loved horse races, and whenever Oriental Park had them, he took us on a weekend day. Oriental Park was located in Marianao, another suburb of Havana. Dad explained that this was a thoroughbred horse racing facility operated by the Havana-American Jockey Club of Cuba. The club was popular, not only among Cubans, but also among Americans and Europeans who visited the island. Dad also explained how to bet and introduced me to some of the horse owners and jockeys. The park was large and beautiful. One section was popular and crowded. Another one was used for special events and private parties, although anyone could sit on its first floor across from the well-manicured lawns to watch the races. The public section was loud and a bit confusing to me. People ran around like maniacs, making bets and yelling at the horses. Dad always went to that section. He felt it was where the true action was. When my mother went with us, she took me to the private section to have some peace and quiet. Mother disliked crowds and loud events. I must say, I preferred the private section too, where I could play on the green lawn without worrying about getting lost in the crowd. My only enticement to go to the public section was to eat a hot dog.

Dad dreamed of owning a horse. He understood well the art of horse racing and knew what horse to bet on. He was not a gambler but enjoyed the sport. It was a treat for him. I tried to follow the game and make sense out of it but got carried away by the action and theatrics. I liked to go to the stables and learned something new listening to dad as he talked with the jockeys, owners, and caretakers when a horse was injured. Dad could diagnose the horse's problem. I always felt he knew so much!

El Vedado had a small amusement park called Jalisco Park with a roller coaster, carousel, crazy cars, and a few other rides. It had food stands that sold snacks and cotton candy. All the kids from my neighborhood went there. In between rides, I ate pink cotton candy and felt the big puff disappear in my mouth in a second. We ran into neighbors and also into some TV personalities who lived in El Vedado and took their kids to the park to play and enjoy the rides at the park. I remember a day when a woman with blonde hair, wearing a very elegant halter dress, a pair of dark sun glasses, and a large fancy purse came up to us to ask my father a question as we waited in line to get into the roller coaster. We thought her dress style was unusual to be at the park and her manner a little extravagant. It turned out she wanted to know where we had purchased the purse I was carrying because her daughter wanted one like mine. Mother told her that we had purchased it at El Encanto. She thanked my parents while flirting a little bit with my dad. "That was Rosita Fornés," said mother. I agreed and looked back to take another peek at Rosita, who was accompanied by her then-boyfriend, Armando Bianchi. They were both popular and well-known Cuban TV stars.

My parents, especially mother, were ready to celebrate my birthday with a traditional party at home. Such a party consisted of inviting one's schoolmates and friends, singing Happy Birthday in English—since Cuba was fast to adopt American customs—cutting a cake, eating pastries and small sandwiches, and drinking Coca-Cola. Friends brought gifts, and we all played games such as hide-and-seek, musical chairs, or pinning the tail on the donkey, blindfolded. At the end, all the kids pulled the strings of a piñata for candy to come pouring down.

When I was to turn seven, I considered having some of my closest friends over for such a party but had a better idea. I wanted to celebrate my birthday with just a few friends at El Carmelo, a fancy restaurant that my family frequented for light dinners or snacks. The restaurant had an enclosed section for dining and an open air terrace where they served sandwiches. El Carmelo was known for a sandwich called Elena Ruz, made with lightly toasted and sliced white bread, filled with strawberry preserves, cream cheese, and slices of roasted turkey. All members of the Cuban and the Anglo-American society frequented the restaurant. I enjoyed their light food fare, for I was not a big eater. I suggested to my parents to have my birthday party there. They agreed, and for the first time, when I turned seven, I had a circle of my closest schoolmates, my cousins and aunts who lived in Havana, and my grandmother and parents join me after school to celebrate at El Carmelo! I felt very gown up.

A few years later, while we were planning to leave Cuba, I was being tutored in stenography and English by Silvia, my older second cousin. She and I stopped by El Carmelo to buy miniature cheese-filled pastries as a treat after class. Eventually, El Carmelo, as we knew it, was confiscated by the Revolution in 1960.

Isabelita, my maternal grandmother, and I went shopping in our neighborhood after I came home from school. We visited Rivero's little shop, which had four glass cases full of knick-knacks, little gifts, batteries, chewing gum, hard candy, and chocolate boxes. The store walls were covered with toys and decorative items for the home. "Come with me to see what we can buy today," grandma said. She and the owners greeted each other exchanging views about the weather, the latest news, and the merchandise that they were expecting. I always walked out with a little gift, or better yet, with a yellow box of Chiclets. Our next stop was the Arellano pharmacy at the corner of our block. The pharmacy was huge next to Rivero's shop. To get to the pharmacy, we passed by various houses on our block, ending in the one owned by a music teacher called María. She had three daughters who always fought with each other. We could hear María's piano when she was teaching a private lesson or her family's arguments, and we also watched her backyard chickens fly into the clean, tree-lined street. The pharmacy owners always chose to ignore María's family, especially her chickens.

I could tell grandma was nearby from the noise of her seven silver bracelets, worn together to represent each day of the week. As soon as I heard her coming, I got ready to beg her to play the store game with me, an early indication that I would enjoy shopping later on in life. Mother's armoire became the shop. Item by item was described to grandma, hoping that she would buy one. Finally, after quite a few attempts, she purchased one item from me. I knew when she was tired of playing by her lack of attention, or the fact that she had fallen asleep. The signal was clear. It was time to close shop.

Grandma lived with us but spent a lot of time at one of her sister's house. She and dad got along well. He admired her budget management skills. Grandma respected dad and sided with him in any arguments he had with my mother, which infuriated mama. Grandma was active until she died, overseeing the maid's chores and our family's weekly menus, while mother worked at the Children and Family Social Services department. Grandma's bangles tinkled whenever she boiled water in our kitchen pantry. She strained the water with a cloth to eliminate any calcification left on the pot. She believed that was the best way to purify our drinking water and never wanted to buy the modern bottled version. Her other regular chore was cleaning our silver. This was a task to be done only by her. She never trusted anyone else with our silver.

Mother and I visited grandma whenever she stayed with her sister Josefina, who we called Pepa. We took a bus to La Sierra, in the neighborhood of Havana known as Marianao, where Pepa lived. Pepa had four sons and two daughters. Two of her sons were well-known society column journalists in Havana. One of her sons was later imprisoned by the Castro regime for helping people persecuted by the Revolution escape through embassies. One of Pepa's daughters, Carmen Susana, worked with disadvantaged people. She frequented the society balls, like her siblings and cousins, but her call in life was clear. Carmen Susana joined the Carmelite Order to become a nun and grade school teacher. She taught me to read and write Spanish in the Teresian School of El Vedado run by the Carmelites and inspired by St. Teresa of Avila. I never thought I would accompany Carmen Susana on the last night she spent in Cuba in her mother's house. At that point she had stopped wearing her nun's habit and was hiding in fear of repression from the Revolution. She and I spent a great part of that night talking about life, faith, and courage and how to face the unknown.

Pepa's house was not large, but was lovely. My favorite places in the house were the library and the backyard. A glass door opened from the living room into the library. Books covered the walls of the room, facing an elegant European desk and chair in the center of the library. Various wicker chairs and Oriental vases adorned the rest of the room. Their narrow dining room had glass doors that opened onto a backyard encircled by bougainvillea. The yard was quiet, cozy, and colorful. Pepa and her sister Amita, my grandmother's twin sister, lived in the house with their old and fragile maid, Catalina, a slim black woman of medium height, who was considered part of the family. Whenever I visited them, Catalina made a special dessert for me, either bread or rice pudding. During my last visit to Pepa's house, when I knew we were leaving Cuba, I talked with Catalina for a long time. She had worked in our household when I was born. I knew we would never see each other again.

There were two versions of Russian meat for me. One version was a tasty dish that we ate at a neighborhood restaurant owned by a woman called Nieves. Little did I know that Nieves's name, which meant "snow" in English would be foretelling of storms that I would face in the future. We visited her restaurant located at the corner of our house and sat at a table on the terrace that wrapped around the ground floor of a pink stucco apartment building. Nieves was a friendly woman in her 40s, tall and thin with light reddish-brown hair. Sunday's specialty was Russian Meat, a roll of baked minced meat topped with a pink and creamy sauce, similar to a Thousand Island dressing. It was absolutely delicious.

The other Russian meat was actually from Russia and started arriving in Cuba a year after Fidel's policies resulted in food and other scarcities for Cubans. At first, we wondered what type of meat it was. It seemed to be American Spam, but we quickly we realized it was not. We found that meat inedible. It was canned, greasy, bland, and smelled of left-over pork grease. Was it safe to eat? We skipped it. Nieves's corner restaurant stayed open but not for long after Fidel took power. Not much food was available, and people did not have money. The government was seizing most of it. Nieves's delicious Russian Meat disappeared. Whenever we asked for the dish, the answer was the same: "Not today." The only Russian meat available was the Russian kind. We never saw Nieves again after we moved from our house on 20th Street to a small apartment while we were getting ready to leave Cuba. We started to lose touch with friends. Many persons already had left and others disappeared. Would we see Nieves again?

TWO

THE TERRACE OF 20TH STREET

Much of our life in Cuba was lived outdoors, not in the countryside or at the beaches, but on its terraces, patios, and courtyards. Houses and apartments had terraces or indoor and outdoor patios, and schools had courtyards. My family frequently used their terrace. It was our ritual, our way to connect with nature while being in the city. What better place to gaze at the blue sky, to feel the evening's breeze, to look for a shooting star or make out the constellations, or to reach for the moon? Our terraces were the centers of our family activities: kids played and relatives caught up with each other while fanning themselves on wicker rocking chairs. We leaned over our balconies to chat with neighbors and call upon street vendors. Our terrace was a member of my Cuban family. Other Cubans enjoyed their terraces too, except for our first-floor neighbors, who always kept to themselves.

Our home was a flat on the second floor of a two-story house in El Vedado, an area initially built outside of Havana as a vacation place for wealthy families that later became an established section of the city. El Vedado developed its own character, with Spanish- and Italian-style houses, tree-lined boulevards, modern apartment buildings, restaurants, shops, and radio and TV stations. Some of its streets were numbered. Ours was 20th Street between 15th and 17th Streets. Other street names were letters such as L and O; yet others had names such as Línea, Paseo, and Calzada.

A black iron fence encircled our building and garden. From our garden, a tiled terrace led to our private stairwell with two large glass windows. We seldom sat in our living room with its pink flamingo walls, mosaic tiled floor, and dark mahogany and wicker furniture except to watch our black-and-white TV across from the Sacred Heart painting on the wall. Later, our TV allowed us to witness what today would be a reality show: how the Cuban Revolution took hold of our island. A long hallway, with doors that opened into each bedroom and bathroom on one side and windows on the other, led to our dining room. The dining room furniture was dark mahogany turned beige by an impulse of my mother, who thought they needed levity. Coraza, a wire-thin black man who was our painter, never said much, but he listened intently to our decorating ideas while smoking his Cuban cigar. His work was always superior to our expectations. Our dining room furniture was turned into an antique beige tone that contrasted with our slightly darker walls and our window's view of Havana's bay. Our pantry and kitchen ended at the maid's quarters, a place that I often visited to chat with Elda, our cook and maid and one of my conspirators in pranks.

Our living room's French doors opened onto our terrace with its semi-open stone verandas, red mosaic tile floor, and wicker rocking chairs. All the activities on our terrace remain in my mind as different fragments of my childhood.

One of the most memorable activities was the daily after-dinner visit of my mother's cousin Cuca and her husband Antón. They lived nearby on 17th Street. We sat with them on the terrace at 7 p.m. I enjoyed being part of their visit, at least for a short while, to hear the latest news, to observe their mannerisms, and to find out what purse and fan Cuca was wearing. She dressed conservatively and finished her attire with a different purse and fan each day. Of all her purses, my favorite one was in the shape of a little box. It was made out of a gray plastic that imitated mother of pearl. Throughout the visit, she opened and closed her fan numerous times, with decisive movements, as if to make a point. I always borrowed her fan, but quickly returned it because I was afraid of breaking it. Cuca's hair had more shades of light blue than gray, thanks to a coloring technique. Her green eyes seemed to smile at you, and her rounded figure was reassuring. She had perfectly manicured hands worthy of admiration.

Cuca's husband, Antón, contrasted her with his olive skin, black hair, and eyes. He liked to wear a white short-sleeved shirt, gray linen or wool pants, and a sweater, depending on the season. A gold watch tucked in his pant's side pocket hung down from a chain.

They talked about family matters, the theatre, music, plays, and about Batista and the rebels. I was interested in that latter part of the conversation. They updated us on acts of terror committed in the city, whether a bomb explosion at a movie house or an attack in a town outside of Havana. They reported which were the safe places to visit and speculated on the odds of the rebels winning against Batista's army. At 9:00 p.m. we would hear *el cañonazo*, a cannon fired every night as a tradition followed since the time that Cuba was a colony of Spain. In colonial times, the cannon alerted the people of Havana to go inside their houses for protection against pirates. We looked at our watches to make sure that we heard *el cañonazo* and not a bomb explosion or a terrorist act committed by Batista's opposition to intimidate the population. At that point, Cuca and Antón got up to leave. Their visit always ended on time, with the 9:00 p.m. fired cannon.

Cuca and Antón owned real estate and businesses. Antón's family owned the most exclusive jewelry store in Cuba, Le Palais Royal, located on Obispo Street in Old Havana. The store, a sophisticated enclave decorated in royal blue and gold, sold diamonds, all types of precious stones, gold, dinnerware, and silverware. Their jewelry designers created unique pieces that were sold at the store or commissioned to them. Their jewelry boxes, designed in royal blue and gold with the store's emblem, were well-known throughout Latin America. Anyone who visited Cuba and was interested in jewelry made a stop at the store for its distinguished reputation.

Mother told me a story about a group of singers from Argentina who visited Le Palais while performing in Havana. They did not purchase a bracelet at Le Palais Royal because they had seen a similar one at another store at a lower price. Le Palais's salesperson explained that the difference was probably because of the amount of 18k gold in the bracelet. Le Palais certified its jewelry to attest that it if was labeled 18k gold, it was completely made out of it. The singers did not make the purchase and bought the cheaper bracelet. A few years later, they visited Havana again and went to Le Palais Royal to tell them that they'd had their bracelet appraised and were told that it was not solid 18k gold but hollow gold.

Cuca and Antón were married when they were nineteen years old. They loved each other and lived without worries, at least not financial ones. They were methodical, logical, refined, and reserved, but caring and responsive to any family member who was in need. The only cloud in their lives was that they could not bear children, something they longed for. When my sister America was born, they were delighted. Somehow they took to thinking that she was the daughter that they'd never had, or their grandchild. My sister, an expressive little girl with curly blonde hair and big brown eyes, also took a strong liking to them. She thought they were the grandparents that she hardly knew.

My sister had lunch with Cuca and Antón on Saturdays. The menu changed every day under Cuca's supervision. After lunch, Cuca provided silver finger bowls filled with water and rose petals for her guests to clean their fingers. My sister loved that routine. The finger bowls left an impression on her as they did on anyone who had lunch or dinner in Cuca's house. One of my mother's cousins, Marcelo, was engaged to a well-to-do young woman from another town in the province of Havana who had lunch at Cuca's house. She did not know about finger bowls. Years later, she told me the story in Miami: "When Marcelo took me to eat at Cuca's house and she put out the finger bowls, I asked him if it was some kind of soup. I was relieved when he told me the bowl was to clean my fingers after the meal. Cuca was so nice and elegant. Ah, those finger bowls. I had no clue then what they were for!" I agreed and laughed.

On weekends, I set up a blackboard at the corner of our terrace to practice spelling with my dad's help. I loved erasing the blackboard, something that I had to give up when the dust caused me to have asthma attacks. It was reassuring to have Dad sitting next to me, leaning back on the rocking chair with his thin, six-foot frame to help me spell. When I was not certain of an answer, he patiently encouraged me to figure things out on my own. He always taught me something new. Dad did not hug or kiss me often, but he showed me his love through the twinkle in his dark eyes and by watching me while I played at the park or by taking me with him to the horse races, his favorite pastime. He was reserved and influenced by his Spanish father.

My paternal grandfather was a Spaniard who lived with his family in Colón, Matanzas, a province of Cuba, east of Havana. Grandfather was a chemist who went to Cuba to avoid Spain's military service. Once in Colón, he built a successful soft drink factory and ended up owning real estate and the movie theatre of Colón. One day, while creating a new flavored soft drink, he badly burned himself in an explosion at the factory. He survived the accident, but his liver was badly damaged. Years later, he was forced to close his factory because of a typhus epidemic. The family moved to Havana, where he became ill. Once he was at the hospital, when it was obvious that he would not recover, my grandmother asked my father to go into the room where Grandfather was dying to say good-bye. That was a moment that my dad never forgot. Grandfather had shaped my father's character and had been teaching him how to manage his business. He had planned to send Dad to the United States to finish high school and learn English. Dad and Grandfather were constantly together and emotionally close.

One day, Dad confided to me that his whole world had stopped and tumbled down when his father died. The family struggled after Grandpa's death, forcing my father, the oldest child, to interrupt his schooling to go to work. His brothers and sisters graduated from Havana University as doctors and teachers. In the meantime, Dad worked and taught himself by reading about geography, history, literature, politics, archeology, and medicine. He also learned English, a language that he loved, by himself. Later, Dad used English when he worked as a general manager of a Cuban–owned manufacturing company that designed, built, and installed professional kitchens and cafeterias in hotels, hospitals, and restaurants. The company had a team of architects and engineers and a manufacturing department that my father created and managed. Little did he know how handy English would be later in his life.

Mother was lively and expressive, with dark wavy hair, hazel eyes, fair skin, and a beautiful figure. She always paid attention to her looks. Mother was attentive to me, but she also played the role of my disciplinarian, because no else in the family did. I did not appreciate that. Sometimes she sat on our terrace to do her nails. I wanted to be her manicurist, but she invariably said no to the idea.

One day, I insisted on doing her nails, but she refused. I suddenly got up from my chair, and the red nail polish bottle broke as it fell on the tiled mosaic floor. The polish splashed all over me, and I got scared, thinking it was blood. I screamed, and my mother became anxious. I realized that I was not hurt, that it was just polish on me and not blood, but now I wanted to scare my mother, who had hurried to my side. Right away, she knew I was fine and scolded me. Her words were final. "You will never do my nails—period. Now help me to clean up this mess. Call the maid and help her too," said Mother.

Although Mother was Cuban, she thought that she was a Spaniard. Father used to kid her about that. Her father, a well-known Spanish lawyer who owned the second-most important law offices in Havana, frequently took the family to Spain, and at one point, permanently moved them to Madrid. Mother and her sister became attached to Spain. Upon Grandfather's sudden death, Grandmother Isabelita, whose family's ascendants were from Spain and France but who had been in Cuba since the 1700s, moved back to Havana, the city she knew best. She missed her family, needed their support, and longed to be near them. She returned to Havana with her two daughters and maid.

Grandmother Isabelita visited with two of her sisters, Pepa and Amita, on our terrace. Pepa and Grandma were in their early seventies and had gray hair, brown eyes, and a little extra weight put on throughout the years. Amita, the other sister and Grandma's twin, was thin, taller, and had expressive green eyes. To keep cool, they dressed in light silk dresses buttoned in front with short sleeves. They talked for hours, having refreshments or iced tea while fanning themselves on their rocking chairs.

Fans were popular in Cuba, and every lady in my family owned a collection. They ranged from the elaborate type, made of mother of pearl with hand-painted scenes, to the cheap style, made of painted cardboard stapled to a piece of wood, the promotional kind businesses gave away. Every female knew how to use the fans for the art of keeping cool while being sophisticated. Grandma, who spoiled me, allowed me to sit on her lap, wearing my dark, large sunglasses, to participate in the visit with her sisters.

While we used our terrace constantly, our first-floor neighbors never used theirs. I thought they were eccentric. We talked with most of the neighbors on our side of the street—especially to María Antonia and her husband Mario, our next door neighbors; to the O'Reilly's, part of that aristocratic family; and to the little store and pharmacy owners—but never with our first-floor neighbors. The wife, an accomplished pianist from Mexico, the husband, a Cuban lawyer, and their two grown sons always kept to themselves. We could hear the lady of the house play the piano every day. I wanted to visit our neighbors, but mother ordered me to respect their privacy and stay away from their front terrace and gardens. Mother let me know that if I disobeyed her, she would punish me.

Warning me of a potential punishment was an enticement to make me do what was forbidden. My mother had that effect on me when I was a child. One day, as I was playing with my fish, I asked Elda, our maid, to help me clean the fishbowl. I wanted to clean it on the dining room's window ledge. Elda warned me that it was risky to do so because one of the fishes could jump and die. I did it anyway. Sure enough, one of the fish jumped and fell downstairs on the neighbor's patio. I was upset and sad and could not control my impulse to rush downstairs to pick up my fish, hoping that it had survived the fall from our second floor. I hurried downstairs by myself and walked into the forbidden territory of our neighbor's property. They never had their windows open, but I was afraid of being watched through the wooden blinds and scolded by them. Truthfully, I was more afraid of what my mother would do for disobeying her. Elda called from our window, "Hurry up and come back. That fish is dead." I brought back my dead fish trying to make it swim to no avail. "I told you it was dead," said Elda.

Elda, a black woman in her late thirties, had a tall, strong, and curvaceous body. She could do any task. Her meals were always tasty and served on time. Her smile and sense of humor were contagious. Elda, my accomplice in my little acts of insurrection, let me into the kitchen reluctantly when she cooked and only allowed me to help her make empanadas.

Elda allowed me to visit her in her quarters. When she was resting, I knocked at her door, asking permission to visit her. I wanted to see how she lived, to peek into her private world apart from us and her household duties. Elda loved us, and we loved her. She took to my sister, América when she was born; she nicknamed her Tatum. When my sister was learning to speak she changed the word *tata*, used in Cuba to refer to a nanny, into *tatum*. Since then, my sister was *tatum* for Elda. América and Elda got along well for many reasons, but especially because América loved the food that Elda cooked, enjoying every bite she took.

When América turned two years old, we had her first birthday party at home among family members and next-door neighbors. Elda helped set the table and did the decorations. She placed the beautiful cake on a low table so that my sister could blow her two candles out. My sister was excited about her party and kept walking by the table to touch the cake platter, trying to eat part of the frosting. Then it happened. She bumped into the table, and the cake fell flat on the floor. América started crying, not knowing how to fix the cake. Along came Elda to clean everything up and fix the cake, which we ended up serving and eating as if nothing had happened.

Before we moved to a small apartment while getting ready to leave Cuba, Elda visited us. We asked her if she was planning to leave too, but she explained that although she would like to, she had too many children to even dream of leaving. I often wondered what happened to her after we left Cuba.

At times, I sat on our terrace to stare at the bright blue sky and fantasize about the universe. Later, as I grew older and heard the news about the revolutionary rebels fighting with Castro against Batista, I looked at the sky and wondered how life would be in Cuba under the rebels' leadership. Our terrace was a great place to dream, but it would not remain so for long once the rebels came down the mountains to the cities, after the triumph of the Revolution.

THREE

CUBAN FOOD

Cuban cuisine had influences from Spain and Europe, Indian tribes who inhabited Cuba before its colonization, Africa, China, and the United States. As a child, I never thought about those food influences; I was just familiar with the food prepared at home by our maid or eaten at our neighborhood's restaurants. Our family's weekly menus included a variety of dishes with fish, poultry, meat, rice, beans, vegetables, and desserts. The menus were planned by my grandmother, and once she passed away, by my mother. Dad selected fresh fish and meat at the market on Sunday mornings, amidst a bustling crowd that he thoroughly enjoyed. I watched him talk to the vendors as he selected the best picks, while I smelled the plucked and cleaned poultry, the meat cuts, and fish displayed on various counters.

I ate sandwiches or Cuban-Chinese food at the neighborhood restaurants that we visited on weekends. Our typical snacks, whenever we visited the restaurant near the Payret movie house, were Midnight Sandwiches and Cuban Sandwiches, or Flying Saucers. At the fancier El Carmelo Restaurant, we ordered the Elena Ruz Sandwich.

Midnight Sandwiches were made with soft egg buns and slices of Swiss cheese, roasted pork loin, and cooked ham. The bread was spread with mayonnaise on one side and mustard on the other. The sandwiches always had a small, thin dill pickle slice to give it a salty flavor. The Cuban sandwich was similar, but bigger, and used Cuban bread, with its light crust and airy consistency. It also had slices of pork loin, Swiss cheese, cooked ham, and a thin dill pickle slice. It was pressed down to melt the cheese and give it a toasty consistency. It was cut diagonally in two halves and served hot. This sandwich was a favorite among Cubans.

I loved eating Flying Saucers at a restaurant near the Payret movie theatre; its name, which I thought creative, made me think of outer space and unknown galaxies. One slice of the white bread was spread with mayonnaise and the other with strawberry preserves, slices of baked ham and Swiss cheese filled the inside. The white bread sandwich was grilled and given a round shape to look like a flying saucer.

Whenever we visited the more sophisticated El Carmelo Restaurant, I ordered the Elena Ruz sandwich, named after a Cuban socialite who frequented the restaurant and asked for this specific recipe. The sandwich was made with a soft egg bun. One slice of bread was spread with cream cheese and the other with strawberry preserve and filled with slices of roasted turkey. It was served at room temperature. Stopping by El Restaurante de 23 meant ordering a Cuban fried hamburger. The patties were smaller than those of a typical hamburger and made of a mix of pork and minced beef seasoned with garlic, onion, oregano, cumin and paprika. The bread was spread with mustard and, in some cases, with ketchup.

Mother did not cook, but she liked to make desserts and bake small bread buns to eat as snacks in the middle of the day. In our last two years in Cuba, she made the bread buns more often. My cousin got on his motorcycle to visit us once the Revolutionary Army took over Catholic schools and he stopped attending classes at the LaSalle High School. He called us ahead of his visit to make sure we had hot little buns to snack on.

Our home meals took the different influences of foreign cuisines and mixed them into each dish, enhancing their flavors. I wandered into our kitchen to watch Elda, our maid and cook, prepare the dishes that we would eat later. Many times I volunteered to help, a gesture not appreciated by her since it just added more complications to her chores. I could not understand why she preferred to work alone instead of being helped. One day, I asked her why I could not help her and she explained it as a matter of fact, "Because you don't know how to cook, I have to teach you, and I don't have time. I have to get the meals done on time for dinner," she said. I resigned myself to handing her some cooking utensils, helping her finish the empanadas or just watching her.

It never crossed my mind why, even when our weather was warm, we served a hot soup as part of our meal. It was just the way it was. There were many kinds of soups, but my favorite ones were chicken soup, with its gentle smell from slowly cooking the chicken stock, and plantain soup, with its unique taste from combining beef stock with fried plantain chips. My grandmother's favorite was garlic soup, with its fragrant aroma from the olive oil and garlic topped with freshly fried bread crumbs. Sometimes, all grandma ate in the evenings were a bowl of soup and a piece of Cuban bread that she dipped in olive oil sprinkled with salt. Along with the soups, we ate many stews. We often made okra stew, with what I realize now was a combination of Cuban and African ingredients. The tender okra simmered with pieces of pork, pepper, lime juice, garlic, tomatoes, sherry, and salt to make a thick blend resulting in a savory dish. My father's favorite was oxtail stew cooked with bell peppers, lime juice, onions, oregano, cumin, sherry, and potatoes. It resulted in a peppery taste responsible for its Spanish name, fiery oxtail. I loved the cornmeal stew that Elda prepared for us. She cooked it with onions, lime juice, salt and pepper, olive oil, and dry sherry, adding pieces of pork and mixing them with fresh tomatoes to add color as a finishing touch. The cornmeal stew got better on Fridays, when crab meat was substituted for pork to comply with the Catholic tradition that required eating fish or seafood that day of the week.

We ate many dishes that mixed rice with fish, seafood, poultry, meat, or beans. Another Friday favorite was rice with squid. The white rice cooked with the squid in its black ink became dark and also savory when garlic, olive oil, green bell peppers, and salt were added to it. This dish was not colorful, but it was tasteful and fulfilling. Every other week, we had codfish. Father bought it at the market, and Elda soaked the codfish for hours to eliminate its salt. She prepared the dish with tomato puree, potatoes, olive oil, onions, garlic, and vinegar until the flaky codfish became alive with its unique flavorful taste. I marveled at the transformation that the cod underwent from a stiff salty piece of fish into a tender dish. There was no better dish to have than chicken with rice. The white rice turned yellow from the saffron that Elda added to color it, cooking it slowly with beer and the other ingredients along with the chicken thighs and breasts until they became soft and easy to pull apart just with the fork. We accompanied this dish with ripe fried plantains and a lettuce and tomato salad dressed with vinegar, oil, and salt. Another favorite dish that we served almost every week at our table was Cuban beef stew. Elda said it was easy to prepare with cubed chunks of boneless beef cooked with bell pepper, garlic, onions, potatoes, capers, paprika, sweet peas, and dry sherry. She always served it with boiled white rice. Our salads were simple, usually made of a few lettuce leaves adorned with slices of avocado and tomato and garnished with olive oil, vinegar, and a bit of salt. The salad was always served as part of the main dish. There were weeks when we ate Old Clothes, a dish consisting of steak hash in tomato sauce. The flank steak was cooked and once it cooled, it was shredded and then simmered in a sauce of tomato, olive oil, salt, pepper, garlic, onions, and bell peppers, and eaten with boiled white rice. I never understood the name of this dish but thought it was clever to think of the shredded meat as a piece of old cloth. Italian style liver was never absent from our food repertoire. The pieces of liver, cooked in olive oil with bell peppers, salt, and onions were eaten with boiled white rice. Whenever I was sick to my stomach, I ate taro root. This root turned gray when cooked or boiled. It was then smashed and served hot. It tasted better with a little olive oil and salt, but it was still bland, and I guess what my stomach needed to get better. We usually ate it at home boiled with a little seasoning or pan fried as fritters.

At Christmas, we always ate roast suckling pig. We celebrated Noche Buena or Christmas Eve with my father's family which meant traveling to Colón in the Matanzas province. The traditional dish was a pig roasted over an open-pit fire in the yard or prepared by a local restaurant for families to take home. The pig was served with Creole mojo, black beans with white rice, boiled yucca with garlic sauce, and a lettuce and tomato salad. For dessert we ate Spanish *turrones*, or desserts made of almonds. There were the soft *turrones*, an almond paste, and the hard *turrones* that could crack your teeth, made with hard almonds in the form of a bar.

Since I was not a big eater and preferred desserts to regular meals, mother learned to make a few recipes with the help of Nélida, who was married to Panchito, my mother's cousin and Cuca's brother. Nélida was Panchito's second wife, a courteous lady who visited us frequently by herself or with her niece and nephew. She always brought us a dessert she made with what I felt were her love and good intentions. She was a good baker who took special care in teaching my mother her recipes. I stood by her side to learn how to bake, and to offer my help, which again was seldom accepted. My two favorite desserts were stuffed chayote and bread pudding. Her chocolate ice cream was more difficult to make, which meant that we had it only when she brought it. It was amazing to me to watch Nélida take a white loaf of sliced bread, mix it with all the other ingredients, and turn it into a delicious bread pudding. She added caramelized sugar to the baking pan before pouring the pudding mass in it. Once the pan was in the oven, I started to track the time, hoping to speed it so that I could decorate the pudding with colorful sugar sprinkles and eat it. Nélida never allowed me to rush her into turning the pudding over until it was cool. That was a wise thing. Making stuffed chayote was an elaborate but rewarding task. Nélida carefully cut out the mass of the chayote and kept the outer shells. She mixed the mass with milk, sugar, salt, eggs, vanilla, and raisins before pouring it into the chayote half shells, finally topping them with grinded crackers, raisins, and almonds before baking them. I waited to eat the *chayotes* while they cooled, a time that seemed to be an eternity. Other desserts served at home came from cans, a custom that became popular in the 1950s. Fruits such as guavas and oranges were canned in syrup and served with pieces of Swiss or cream cheese and salty crackers. Other times, we made some popular desserts such as sweet custard, rice pudding, French toast, and sweet potato paste.

When I visited my uncle Lázaro's family in the beach resort of Varadero we went fishing with some of my cousins and a fisherman who lived in the area. We caught white fish, which we cleaned and fried in olive oil on a campfire by the sea, adding just salt and lemon to season it. We sat on a wooden bench, facing the blue sea, eating our fish with a soda or Coca-Cola, before heading back to uncle's home. My appetite grew when I was in Varadero, something that rarely happened to me in Havana, and probably was a result of all the swimming and walking that I did at the beach. After a long day of playing with my cousins and friends, we ate together before the adults ate. That was a custom that I did not like since in Havana I sat at the table with all the adults. One of my favorite dishes was ground beef cooked in olive oil with onions, green bell peppers, garlic, tomato sauce, olives, and raisins mixed with white boiled rice and topped with two fried eggs, sunny side up. Adding the eggs was a tradition at my uncle's that I found odd at first, but got used to quickly and missed once I was back home in Havana. Uncle Lázaro also boiled cans of condensed milk until the milk became thick and slightly brown in color to have as dessert.

Any cool evening in El Vedado provided the excuse to have hot chocolate with *churros*, a Spanish dunking pastry in the form of a long strip fried and sprinkled with powder sugar. We bought this freshly made pastry at a shop or street corner cart bringing it home to dunk in the hot chocolate. This pastry brings back fond memories of our family snacking together at home on a cool evening, or after Midnight Mass during Christmas. On the other hand, summer days lent themselves to having a tropical fruit shake. I loved those thick shakes made from the pulp of the wide variety of Cuban fruits: mango, anones, papaya (my favorite with its red pulp) and guanábana. Milk and sugar were added to the mix. A fruit shake was the accompaniment of choice for a Cuban sandwich, Elena Ruz, Midnight Sandwich or Flying Saucer.

FOUR

CHARACTERS, STREET VENDORS, AND POPULAR CULTURE

Every day I took the same route to school from 20th Street. I turned left on 17th Street and went straight to the Teresian School, making one stop on 18th Street to pick up my younger female cousin. I waited for her at the corner while she left her house in a hurry to meet me. She was four years younger than me, and I was supposed to protect her on the way to school. It was important to walk together around December 4th, the feast day of Saint Barbara, revered by the Catholic Church and Cubans. Rumors were that some persons who practiced Santería kidnapped kids to sacrifice them to the pagan god identified with the Catholic saint. We were not sure that the rumors were true, but walked together and watched everyone carefully around that day. Our instructions were to yell and run if approached by a stranger around December 4th.

After school, once I dropped off my cousin, I stopped at Patricio's, a small and dilapidated café. It was next to the Arellano Pharmacy, where my family bought all their medications and whose owners were our good friends. The café's awning covered its few tables and chairs. Patricio, an Italian of medium height with a head full of curly salt-and-pepper hair and a long curled mustache, was pleasant but distant. He dressed in gray or black pants and a white short-sleeved shirt. The store's glass counters displayed many cookie jars. Patricio sold drinks such as Cuban coffee, café au lait, Cuban refreshments, Coca-Colas, and snacks. The only thing I purchased at the café was an oval chocolate-covered cookie, wrapped in colorful foil paper and called Little African. Patricio always saved two for me. After eating the cookies, I made paper balls with their wrappers, adding the new balls to a collection that I compared with those of my friends.

I wondered how Cuba's small Chinese population ended up in the country. Father explained that most Chinese laborers arrived on the Island in the nineteenth century to build railroads and work the mines. After the Industrial Revolution, many of those laborers stayed in Cuba because they could not afford return passages to China. We had the traditional Chinese laundry in my neighborhood. Whenever I walked by it, I peeked inside with curiosity. I could see a patio, behind the laundry, where the men rested and ate. They sat on wooden stools, facing a small square dinner table, eating out of a bowl with chop sticks. Whenever I stood there looking, they stared back at me, making me run. They kept their ways in the middle of our own society. Everyone depended on them for their laundry.

We visited the Chinese restaurant on 23rd Street on weekends. Their food was delicious, a combination of Chinese dishes with a touch of Cuban flavors. We bought peanuts from a thin, short, and aging Chinese man on weekdays. He walked the streets of our neighborhood calling out, "Oh, peanuts!" Whenever I heard him, I rushed to our terrace to see him. Mother always helped him by buying some peanuts, even though she never allowed me to eat them because the vendor was not too clean. We never knew his name and always referred to him as "Oh, peanuts."

Modesto, a mulatto man, sold desserts out of a red tin box secured with two leather straps, on the streets of El Vedado. He walked down the street calling out, "Desserts, I bring desserts!" As soon as I heard his voice, I alerted my grandmother and mother. We called Modesto from our balcony, and he climbed up the stairs to our flat to meet us in our living room. I eagerly waited as he opened the box and showed us each tray full of delicious desserts: vanilla and chocolate cakes, cookies, caramel milk squares, cappuccino cakes, and meringues. They were freshly made and at a good price. We selected our favorite desserts and ate them as afternoon snacks. We never heard Modesto's voice announcing his presence and tasty desserts after the rebels won. I missed him more than the desserts and wondered what happened to him.

I never saw the Gentleman from Paris in person, but was intrigued by his persona. He walked around Havana on sidewalks made of small colorful mosaics like the sidewalks of Rio de Janeiro. He wore a dark cape, had a long beard and hair, and carried books under his arms. Was he Cuban or French? Had he been rich and lost his fortune? Was he mad? I never knew. He was one of Havana's treasured presences and mysterious legends. He was a deep contrast to all other Cubans who usually dressed in light or bright colors because of the weather. He seemed happy, an erudite disconnected from Cuban society. What happened to him after the Revolution? Someone said they built him a statue after his death.

I was amazed by a bizarre story based on true facts. A woman in Havana walked down Prado and Neptuno, two popular and crowded streets, wearing only a transparent rain coat and carrying an umbrella. Everyone was shocked and kept talking about it. This was a scandalous thing to do and against all morality. I heard the story in our terrace during the nightly visits of Cuca and Antón and asked to see her photos. Mother said that the woman was obviously not well-balanced and no, there were no photos to show me. Later on, a song about this incident became a hit. Its title was *The Deceitful One from Prado and Neptuno*.

My parents frequented Tropicana, the world-renowned Havana nightclub whose décor was copied in Las Vegas and Paris. It was located in Marianao, a suburb of Havana. I dreamt of visiting Tropicana when I got older, but as a child I could only imagine it or watch television shows that resembled its famous dancing acts. I imagined Tropicana full of smartly dressed couples, dancing and sipping popular drinks. I dreamt about all this while I listened to the stories waiting for my time to go, but it never came.

I went to other shows that I did not dream about, but thoroughly enjoyed. My parents took me to see a popular Spanish singer, who was the rave in Havana in the late 1950s. His name was Pedrito Rico; he had a beautiful face, almost too beautiful to be masculine, and exaggerated mannerism. His short and thin figure moved quickly and effortlessly as he sang songs from Andalusia and danced flamenco. I memorized the lyrics of his songs, which I read in his *cancionero*, a magazine that his promoters sold with his pictures, life story and songs. Another *cancionero* that I owned was that of Sarita Montiel. She was another big name from Spain who was popular in Cuba. Sarita made musical movies where she sang Spanish couplets. I loved her low and melodious voice and her poignant interpretation of the song's lyrics. Her movies were always about love and betrayal. She played the role of a poor young woman who got ahead with her beauty and talent for acting and singing but also with help from a rich man. It was implied that she would have succeeded no matter what because she had great talent. The man who was the lead male part never married her because his social position would not allow it. In some cases, when the man challenged his family and friends for his love, either he or Sarita would die. Sarita had a perfect face, with big almond-shaped caramel-colored eyes and sensuous lips, dark hair, fair skin, and a well-shaped figure. I liked watching her hand movements when she sang. Her fingers were long, and her oval manicured nails in a pale color looked totally natural. One night sitting in our terrace, my mother's cousins, Cuca and Antón, started to tell us about the Sarita Montiel show that they had seen. Since I liked Sarita, I began to pay attention to the adult conversation. They started saying that the show was good, well-attended, that Sarita performed her couplets with a melodious voice and wore a beautiful low-cut dress. "Her breasts looked like two *guanábanas* (a round fruit) ready to fall out," said Cuca. I started to think how that would happen and laughed to myself. I had never heard Cuca make such a remark. She was always so proper.

I watched television in the afternoons while I was doing my homework; somehow I concentrated better with the TV's noise in the background. I turned the TV on when the American cartoons of Tom & Jerry and Mickey Mouse were on. I always finished my homework on time and got good grades, so my mother never said anything about this habit. Saturday mornings were more relaxed and allowed me to watch Betty Boop, Flash Gordon, Laurel and Hardy, The Three Stooges, and Greta's silent movies with Spanish subtitles. I loved the cowboy and Indian movies and *I Love Lucy,* because Ricky was Cuban, and Lucy was so funny.

Some evenings my parents and I watched La Tremenda Corte or the tremendous court on TV. Nananina, one of the characters in the show, would make a complaint to the judge about another character called Three Skates. A misunderstanding of words and intentions were at the core of the comedy, and the judge, who had to interpret the situation, invariably fined Three Skates.

I watched boxing with my dad and soap operas with my mom on television. The soap operas or *novelas* were my favorite; I could not stomach boxing too well. As I grew older, I developed a crush on the young leading men of the soap operas. They were in their late teens or twenties and older than me, but that did not impede my falling in love with them. We liked to watch a live show called *The Waxed Pole*, where someone from the audience was selected to climb a waxed pole with bare hands and feet. If the man made it to the top and took the flag, he would win a prize such as a mattress, a refrigerator, or some other appliance. Well-known brand products sponsored the show. Another branded product, a soap detergent called Jabón Candado or "lock soap" also gave away prizes. If you found a rooster in the detergent box, you could even win a house. The house would have the logo of Jabón Candado on the front door as an advertisement for the soap brand.

Our TV commercials had popular jingles and slogans that everyone sang or recited by heart. Fab soap promised to make bubbles and foam to clean your clothes. Its slogan said, "You have to have faith because everything arrives," referring to the end product of perfectly clean clothes that you could get only with Fab. This advertising slogan was later used to refer to the Revolution, which had finally arrived. A popular beer, Crystal, used a line that everyone repeated "Are you having fun? Of course, if Crystal is present, you are having fun." And lastly, there was Hatuey, the beer named after an Indian martyr during the Spanish conquest. Hatuey was the great beer from Cuba, and everybody liked it. Cuban housewives watched the Frigidaire Kitchen for recipes, and they relied on the instructions given by the show's star, Ana Dolores Gómez, a famous cooking teacher who became a TV personality with this show.

Live TV programs transmitted performances of well-known American and European singers, such as Nat King Cole and Domenico Modugno, who sang "Volare." They also featured Latin stars, such as Louis Aguile, a Chilean teenage idol; Carmen Miranda, the Brazilian bombshell; and Libertad Lamarque, a refined Argentine film star and singer. Cubans liked to watch singers such as René Cabel, Olga Guillot, Celia Cruz and Beny Moré on television. Various orchestras' shows were also popular, such as those of the Sonora Matanzera, Fajardo and His Stars, and Orefiche.

FIVE

THE TERRACE OF TÍA CARMEN LUISA AND THE PATIO OF TÍA MARÍA

We lived near Aunt Carmen Luisa's house, a modern building with four apartments. Hers was on the first floor with a terrace in front and a garden in back. It faced 18th Street. We visited her every other day after school. Her first floor neighbors had two children, Carmen, a little girl, and Osvaldito, a blond boy with soulful eyes, two years younger than me, who was a paraplegic. An attentive and compassionate teenage nanny took care of him. I went over to my aunt's neighbor's apartment to talk with Osvaldito and his nanny, who became my friend even though she was older than me. Osvaldito loved my attention, laughed at my jokes, and looked at me adoringly. Every visit made me feel closer to him. It pained me to see his stiffness and his inability to control his body, even though he had such a clear and intelligent mind. His parents appreciated the time I took to be with him whenever I visited my aunt.

At Aunt Carmen Luisa's, my cousins and I played together while Osvaldito's father carried him so that he could run and play with us. We tied our younger male cousin to a rocking chair and when he yelled in panic, we let him go. I crossed the street to play hide and seek in the neighborhood with the two boys who lived in the big house. Other days we placed a bucket of water on top of the garden fence, tied it to a tree with an invisible thread, and watched passersby get wet. They never knew where the water had come from. We ran to a nearby apartment building where Raquel Revuelta, a well-known actress, lived and knocked on her door. Whenever she answered, we ran away, lacking the nerve to ask for her autograph.

Aunt Carmen Luisa had many visitors. Two of her cousins regularly stopped by her house. One of them, Carina, was a fashionable dresser with dark almond-shaped eyes and a perfect smile.

I admired her interesting jewelry, especially her gold bracelet full of large and unique charms. She smoked in a sophisticated way, the only way society women did, holding her cigarette with her long thin fingers with polished red nails. After an hour, she would leave to go play bridge with her friends. Then Susi, the other cousin, arrived. This one was more beautiful than Carina, with an angelic face and a perfect body, but was unaware of her looks. She smoked a lot. She was married for the second time to her first husband, whom she loved, but the marriage did not work out. She had many admirers but never married again.

After the Revolution triumphed, we regrouped less and less in aunt's terrace. We were busy making plans to leave the country. My family had to leave our beloved flat on 20th Street and move to a small apartment. Unexpectedly, Osvaldito passed away from pneumonia. His death broke my heart. Our routine ended.

Aunt María's house was nice and located in Almendares, another section of Havana. It was part of a row of homes that were two stories high, made out of stucco with front and back yards, and garages attached to them. Aunt María, one of my father's sisters, and her husband, Estrada, had one daughter, Carmencita, on whom they dotted, but who they kept under strict rules. They loved and overprotected her. It seemed that, to them, there were no other children but Carmencita. My aunt, who was a teacher, and her husband, a lawyer, worked hard and always made improvements to their house. They eventually expanded the second floor to add a third bedroom that opened to a terrace. They built a maid's room and bathroom on the first floor with access to their backyard. Once the Revolution took hold, they stopped having a maid, and her room was used by a distant cousin, Cuco, who moved to Havana. He was developmentally delayed, but was a helpful hand and had a good soul. Cuco ran errands for Aunt María and her husband, and cleaned their patio and car to earn his living in their house. The sun porch next to the dining room had access to the patio through a separate door. This was my favorite room in the house because it conveyed a light and happy feeling with its glass venetian-style windows and wicker furniture. The rest of the house had a formal, somber, and heavy style, like Estrada's personality.

We sat on the white iron patio furniture of their backyard that faced a huge mango tree. Their patio was encircled by a fence, but one could still see and talk with their neighbors whenever they opened their second story windows. We gathered in the backyard to play, run around, and shake the leaves of the mango tree to catch and eat a mango as an afternoon snack. Other days, my mother, aunts, and cousins spent a day in the park near the Almendares River, where we sat near the rocks to have picnics.

When Isabelita, my maternal grandmother, became ill, my parents sent me with my sister and our maid to stay at Aunt María's. We slept together in one of the upstairs bedrooms. Our maid had a reserved and bitter temperament. She was a relatively young, thin mulatto woman. I disliked her because I felt that we could not trust her. One night, as we were trying to fall asleep, I asked her if she had any news about my grandmother's health since my parents would not tell me anything. I asked if she was getting better. She turned to me and with a sly smile said, "Your grandmother is dying and you will probably never see her again." I was nine years old and at that moment I realized for the first time how evil some people could be. Why could she not say the truth in some other way? She was glad that I was in pain, I could tell. It became clear to me that she resented and hated my family.

The following day, my sister América, who was almost two years old, and I were playing in Aunt María's patio. My little sister was busy picking up things from the patio floor. I noticed that she had something in her mouth. I asked her to show me what it was but at first she would not. I finally said in a strict tone, "Show me what you have in your mouth!" She spit a glass marble from her mouth. She had found it on the patio. It was dirty and she was trying to chew on it to swallow it! I took it out of her mouth and walked over to our maid, who was supposed to be watching us, but especially my sister, and I said, "Aren't you supposed to be taking care of my sister? Isn't that your job while we are here? Look at what she could have swallowed. She would have choked and died! "Our maid did not care. She was negligent and bitter. When mother came to see us that day I told her what had happened. She reprimanded the maid. When we finally returned home, I told mother that she had to fire our maid. Mother was puzzled and asked me to give her my reasons. I told her that our maid did not appreciate us and resented us and that she did not take good care of us. Grandmother already had died, but I never told mother what our maid said. I did not want mother to be more upset than she was. My mother fired the maid, and then Elda came to work in our house.

I was not allowed to go to my grandmother's funeral, although I asked permission to do so. I think that it was a mistake my parents made out of good intentions. Children understand death, and in my case, I needed to be near my grandmother once more. Mother thought it would be too harsh for me to attend the funeral and burial. Children just did not attend such events in Cuba.

SIX

VACATIONING ON BEACHES
AND IN OTHER CITIES

I looked forward to the sound of the passing train when we stayed at the house of a paternal aunt by the Bay of Matanzas. My sister was not born yet. My parents and I slept together in a large bed on the second floor bedroom. I heard the train that passed nearby early in the morning as the sun's light pierced through the window. Its sound finally woke me as I looked once more through the high window to catch the fullness of the morning sun. I knew that soon we would get up to have breakfast, a large cup of *café au lait* with Cuban bread and butter. I loved the aroma of freshly brewed coffee and the melting butter on the toasted bread. Later in the day, my cousin and I played on the swings of the backyard facing the bay. Once we got tired, we left the yard to pick up seashells by the shore. At night, we caught light bugs that we kept in a large crystal jar with a metal lid full of holes so that they could breathe. We used the jar as our night lantern when we walked in the dark yard. We kept the light bugs for one night, setting them free in the morning to start catching new ones all over again.

My mother and her family visited the popular beaches of Havana while my father's family preferred Varadero Beach, in the province of Matanzas, where they grew up. Mother vacationed in Santa Fé, Tarará, and Guanabo. Luis, one of her cousins, owned a house in Tarará, a gated and beautiful resort in Eastern Havana with art deco houses. However, Tarará's waters were treacherous, and I almost drowned in them when an underground current pulled me down while swimming. Mother loved Santa Fé, a beach town just outside of Havana City, and had toyed with the idea of moving us there. We never moved and kept living in El Vedado.

Aunt Carmen Luisa, mother's sister, took me with her family and friends to spend some Sundays in Guanabo, another beach resort in

Eastern Havana with small villas and hotels. We spent the day at a public club where we ate and swam in its sea. We ate Cuban hamburgers and fresh fried fish in the open air restaurant and bar. The children drank refreshments and the adults Cuban beers. We watched the public dance to popular Cuban songs of the time: a romantic bolero or lively cha-cha-cha. Some days we played the juke box, and others we enjoyed the live music from the band. I liked the sea and sand and the food, but mostly I liked Guanabo's simple ways.

Summer was my favorite season in Cuba. For foreigners, the change in seasons may not have been too obvious, but for the locals the change was noticeable. Winter required that we wear sweaters and wool jackets. Some fancy society women wore furs to special events, probably as a way to show off status and wealth. Spring was rainy, and fall was dry. I looked forward to going back to school in the fall after having enjoyed the summer activities that took me away from Havana and closer to nature. On one hand, I found Havana overpowering with its bustling crowds, and on the other hand, I found it constricting with its social rules.

My parents did not belong to a private club in Havana like some of our other maternal relatives and instead bought a series of passes to El Profesional, a club mostly frequented by professionals. We visited the club in the summer months to go swimming, play on the sand, and eat lunch with Aunt Carmen Luisa and her daughter. One day, as I jumped into the pool with my life preserver in the shape of a doughnut, I slipped right out of it since I was thin. I vividly remember how scared I was when I noticed that I was sinking all the way to the bottom of the pool. I wondered if mother could see what happened and would come to my rescue. She was in the pool. I could not see or hear anything, so I thought that I was on my own. I stopped breathing as I kept sinking down, thinking that if I had gone down, I could go up if I relaxed, touched bottom, and pushed myself up with all my strength. I did not know how to swim, but quickly learned at that moment. I came out of the water to see my mother's pale and relieved face. She was in the pool with someone who was trying to find me. I explained to her that I had not held on to the life preserver as I dove in. She bought me another life preserver after this event, an orange jacket that I had to strap around my legs, arms, and chest. I did not like it, but it made me feel safer.

Every summer I drove with my cousin's family to Varadero, a beautiful seaside resort with pink oleander flowers and clean fine white sand facing the blue sea. Varadero was a town that had a modest neighborhood where local workers and fishermen lived but also had grand hotels and luxurious homes, including the Dupont estate. The Hotel Kawama, built from stones, had a surrounding complex of beachfront bungalows and cabanas. A large bar and veranda offered panoramic views of the ocean. It was a popular place to socialize, have lunch, swim and go dancing. Another popular place was La Bolera, a rustic outdoor ballroom with a thatched roof, built on the beach. One of our favorite pastimes was to go bowling at the old fashioned bowling alley with my younger cousins and their nannies. In those days, new apartment buildings were being built a few blocks from the sea and were being bought by Cuban professionals like my uncles. Varadero also had popular regattas where yachting clubs such as El Club Náutico de Varadero competed with other clubs. Despite some of its glamour, Varadero was and remained a family resort town.

The drive by car to Varadero was pleasant. We left Havana through a tunnel leading to la Vía Blanca, a modern road built by Batista that took us straight to the beach in two-and-a half hours. From our car, we enjoyed the Cuban landscape full of green vegetation, medium sized hills, and tall and gracious palm trees.

An activity I enjoyed in Varadero was hunting for iguanas. This activity was more imaginary than real and was led by my older cousin. We went out driving with our uncle Lázaro to eat fried fish by the sea in an unpopulated area. My cousin and I walked around in a section of the beach full of low hills and green bushes while the fishing and cooking took place. The pathways that we took were rocky and full of weeds. "Iguanas are around. Let's catch some," said my cousin. "What do they look like? Do they bite?" I asked. My cousin described their look, confirming that they could bite. "Well, I'm afraid of them," I said. "Oh, don't be silly. You're bigger than them," he replied. "All right, but you go first," I answered in fear. One afternoon, we finally found one iguana, but it ran away from us faster than we could move. That was the end of our hunting adventure. We walked down the hill, tired of waiting for another iguana, but ready to eat the fried fish my uncle and his fishermen friend had caught for us. They cooked the entire fish on a skillet over a camp fire. We ate out of tin dishes and drank water and Coca-Cola bought at a small cantina stand. The sea was beautiful, the sun was burning, and the sand was hot. We sat at wooden benches near the cantina to enjoy our meal before heading back to town to my uncle's apartment.

While we were in Varadero, Uncle Lázaro, an orthopedic surgeon, was busy during the week working in Cárdenas, where he was the director of its main hospital. On summer evenings and weekends, he joined us to entertain friends, swim in the sea, and go fishing. Sometimes his fishing expeditions were not in the deep sea, but at a deck by the deep waters where he caught baby sharks. He took his three daughters and me with him. One day, we drove to a secluded section on the top of a hill. From there, we walked down to be met by his fisherman guide at the pier. To be safe, he made us stay behind by the sand and grass to watch him fish from afar. That day uncle got lucky and caught a baby shark. It was difficult to do so. We were enchanted by the whole physical beauty of that area, a favorite fishing spot of Hemingway, and by the danger of catching a shark. My uncle brought the baby shark back with him to show everyone. He left it on the ground next to the garage. I felt bad for the shark. What a waste. We did not even try to eat it.

To arrange for a fishing expedition in Varadero, uncle Lázaro took us to visit the fisherman who would lead him. His house was in the section of town where all other fishermen and construction workers lived. Their blonde and tanned children were always running around barefooted but clean. I remember the fisherman's house being small with a portico. The fisherman invited us in to have Cuban coffee. We walked onto his nice living room furnished with a TV set and sofa and then onto his small dining room where we sat to drink the coffee made by his wife. For the first time I drank *café carretonero*, meaning that they left the coffee grounds in to settle at the bottom of the cup. I did not like that type of Cuban coffee but enjoyed the fisherman's family.

As I grew up, I started to go out in Varadero with my cousin and his friends. They were a few years older than me, and they taught me how to dance, a must in Cuban society. I went with them for rides in their speed boats and for drives in their MGs. I felt happy because even though I was younger, they let me tag along with them, making me feel like a grown-up teenager.

One Saturday my cousin said there was a big dance at Kawama's Hotel, and that they were all going. "Do you want to come?" he asked. I said yes. I already knew one of my cousin's friends, Cornelio, whose nickname was Pupy, was going to be there. I had a crush on Pupy, a fourteen-year old boy of medium height with large green eyes who was always tanned. Unfortunately, he had a crush on Sarita, a pretty fifteen-year old girl who already had a woman's figure. I was skinny, did not wear any make-up at that time, and did not have outfits like the older girls wore, but I was tall for my twelve years of age and ventured out. This was my first and only teenage party in Cuba. I had a lot of fun dancing by the sea in the beautiful open terrace of Kawama's Hotel and never forgot the party. Once there, unexpectedly, I ran into another older male cousin of mine, Raulito, who lived in Havana and was vacationing there. He was on my mother's side of the family and in his late teens. He was surprised to see me dancing since he knew my age. I did not care. I thought he would not be able to tell my parents that I was there, and anyway, I was just having fun. I told him I had come with my other cousin. He looked for him and after seeing him with us, relaxed. We kept on dancing and having a good time.

I had a chance to talk to Pupy alone. I knew he liked me just as a friend and that most of the time he did not even notice me, but I took the opportunity to talk to him. He realized that I liked him and kissed me on the cheek. I almost died. "Oh well, at least he kissed me," I thought. Then my cousin arrived and we had to quickly separate from each other. After the dance, we went back to my uncle's apartment where Uncle Lázaro was waiting for us. He was furious because it was almost 1:00 a.m. He gave us a long discourse on why he could not trust us. He thought that we had gone to a friend's house and had no idea that we had gone to Kawama. Under no circumstances were we to do that again. If we ever went to another party, we had to tell him where we were and be home no later than 11 p.m. He explained that he was responsible for our safety. We could tell that our little escapade had terribly upset him and decided never to do it again or risk being banned from his apartment forever.

Vivien, uncle Láraro's youngest daughter, got a pony for her birthday when she turned six. They kept the pony on the backyard of their apartment building, something not unusual since Varadero was not too developed at that time. One afternoon, Vivien decided to go for a ride on her pony without letting anyone know. All of a sudden, we were looking for her and could not find her or the pony. What could have happened? Varadero was a safe place, but we were concerned. Edilia, her mother, finally thought of going to a neighbor's house and found her there talking with them and showing off her pony. Needless to say, the pony was put on sale by my uncle shortly after that.

A fun day at Varadero Beach was when my young cousins and I got drunk without planning it. My parents came to take me back to Havana because school was to start soon. My uncle and aunt gave a small party for family and friends. All the kids finished eating while the adults were having cocktails. We volunteered to take the daiquiris from the kitchen bar to the balcony where the adults were sitting talking and drinking. Every time we took a drink, we took a sip out of its glass. By the end of the afternoon, we were all happy and drunk. I thought we hid it well from our parents until one of my cousins got sick and threw up. That was the last time that we were allowed to carry alcoholic beverages from the bar to the balcony.

When I visited Cárdenas, the town where Uncle Lázaro lived, I stayed at their house, which dated back to colonial times. Two huge doors, wide enough for a horse and carriage to go through, opened into the hallway. Uncle modernized the entrance of the house, where he built a medical office for his private orthopedic practice. Eventually, he also built a modern garage next to the office. Once inside the house and past the waiting room and living room, one found a series of bedrooms on one side. Each bedroom had doors and windows that opened to an enclosed terrace and patio. The dining room and kitchen were on the back and wrapped around the patio. The servants' quarters were upstairs and had a balcony that overlooked the enclosed patio. At night we slept with nets over our beds because Cárdenas was full of mosquitoes in the evenings. When I visited Cárdenas and my uncle was not home, I liked looking around in his office, where I always found the casts he had removed from patients. It was not unusual to find a leg or arm cast on the floor.

SEVEN

THE COURTYARD OF THE TERESIAN SCHOOL

We looked forward to passing the sixth grade. It was a tough school year that prepared us to enter a five-year program before going to the university, or to enter a three-year program before going to the School of Commerce. I attended the Catholic Teresian School, founded by the strict Spanish order of the Carmelites, who followed St. Teresa of Avila's teachings. People said that if you did not learn at this school, you would never learn. We anxiously awaited the break periods to play, run, and buy Coca-Cola in shapely glass bottles out of a vending machine. We shook the bottles until a beige foam appeared inside, took off the caps, and spilled the drinks on each other, staining our carefully ironed white linen shirts.

The Teresian School building took three fourths of an entire city block. Its architectural style was Spanish with Moorish touches, and its beige stucco walls were adorned with brownish designs in the shape of a clover. Low fences surrounded the building and its well-manicured garden full of bougainvillea and small bushes. A few wide steps led to the main door that opened onto a lobby, where one found an office to the right, next to a large glass display case containing rosaries and small religious figures for sale. To this day, I own a Missal in Spanish and Latin and a small marble statue of Christ that I bought from the nuns. Past the lobby, one found an open patio surrounded by long corridors of marble floors. The building's three floors, its corridors, and balconies looked down to the central open patio on whose floor the school's initials STJ (Saint Teresa of Jesus) were engraved. In the basement, the nuns gave free classes to disadvantaged students, held special school functions, taught ballet classes, and conducted choir practices.

Our uniforms, checkered jumpers with matching beanies, linen blouses, and two-toned shoes, used the schools colors of brown, beige and white. Since Cuba had two seasons, summer and winter, we wore light cotton or linen in the summer, and light wool in the winter. A brown wool jacket, with the school's initials, was our protection against the mild winds of winter.

We started our school day marching to a military tune and forming a file in the central patio before going into our classroom. We attended Mass every week, and on the day we took Holy Communion we fasted and ate breakfast in school after Mass. The school's chapel faced the courtyard. Its central aisle led to the altar. Rows of dark brown wooden benches covered the rose marble floors of the chapel. In that chapel, I took my first Communion, after much preparation in our Catechism room and went through the Confirmation rite. The chapel was part of our religious life and education. After Communion, we went to the basement to have chocolate milk in a small glass bottle, accompanied by a piece of soft round bread.

The school was close to our home, approximately four blocks away. During my first few grades, mother walked me to the school and picked me up. One morning, as we started to walk together, mother noticed some puddles of water on the sidewalk from the previous night's storm. She warned me not to step on them. That was the signal that I needed to jump into the puddles and splash my feet in the cold dirty water, getting my shoes and socks completely wet. Mother grabbed my hand and pressed it, telling me to stop. "You are a little devil," she said. I hated when she called me "little devil." She proceeded to explain that as a result of this act and for having disrespected my aunt a few days earlier, I had to stay in school after class as punishment for misbehaving. I was tired after a full day of classes and wanted to go home. Staying after school meant eating with the school boarders instead of enjoying dinner at home, not being able to watch TV while I did my homework, and not going to our terrace in the evening. Dinner at school was followed by two more hours of work under the supervision of Sister Carmen Susana, my mother's cousin. The evening of my punishment, mother came to pick me up around seven. She first talked to Sister Carmen Susana in a low voice. I watched their gestures, but could not hear what they were saying. Mother asked me if I was ready to go home and behave myself. I said that I loved staying in class with the boarders after school. "Very well. You will then stay another day since you like it so much," she said. And so I did. After two days of after-school punishment I had to admit the truth. I never jumped into another puddle of water again when mother took me to school.

When my sister was born, I went to school in the school bus, but I hated to do so because riding the bus made me sick. I asked mother to allow me to walk to school by myself. She did not like that idea and said that she would allow me to do it if I picked up my younger cousin on the way and walked together. We agreed, and for the rest of my years at the Teresian School, my cousin and I walked together to and from school.

The nuns taught ballet classes, which my sister took since first grade, and held choir practices and special school performances in the school basement. They also taught free classes to children of all races and of low-income families who could not pay the schools' tuition or buy uniforms. We had choir practices every week. I loved to sing but had no voice. Sister Milagros, our choir director, said that I could not be in the choir anymore because I sang out of tune. Her decision troubled me because I enjoyed being part of the choir with my classmates and being at the singing practices. I also wanted my parents to see me singing in the choir. An idea came to me and I ended up making an offer to Sister Milagros to stay. I proposed that I could just mimic the words but not sing. She laughed and agreed. I was able to be part of the performance that our school gave to parents. And a great performance it was in the small auditorium located in the lower level. To this day, whenever I hear one of the songs we performed, I get nostalgic as my memories take me to that stage with classmates surrounding me, Sister Milagros directing us, and our proud parents watching the performances. Later, I told my parents about my agreement with Sister Milagros, and they laughed. "You should have continued with your piano lessons instead," said my mother.

Our school had an outdoor patio on the back of the building fenced in by walls and a large wood and iron door. Stands on one end looked toward a field where we played kickball and soft ball. Apartment houses surrounded our patio. Neighbors went out into their balconies to watch us play after school and to cheer for us. We wore our blue culotte skirts, white cotton short-sleeve blouses, and white tennis shoes to attend our gym classes and play kickball.

During Mass the nuns asked us to help with the prayers by reading passages and leading the rest of the participants to provide group answers. I was selected to help one day while in fifth grade. Sister María asked me to sit by the microphone to lead the prayers.

I turned towards the nun surprised and asked her for instructions on what to do. "Just read aloud and wait for the answers," she said. I started reading while she stood next to me, asking me to read louder, which only made me more nervous. "But I am speaking on the microphone. They should hear me," I said. "It doesn't matter; no one can hear you," she replied. My head started to feel dizzy, my nerves took hold of me, and I had to say that I could not read, for I was feeling ill. That was the last time that Sister María asked me to read during Mass. She was a severe-looking nun from Spain who always called me by my full name, María Francisca, not by my nickname, Marietta, which all the others nuns used. I always thought that she was bitter and tired, so after the incident at the chapel, I decided to stay out of her way.

Carmen was my best friend in the sixth grade. We spent time talking and studying together. She was very fair and blue-eyed with dark brown hair. All her siblings had the same look. Her parents were a Spanish couple who owned a successful grocery chain. Once the Revolution started to make drastic changes, they sent their three children to Spain. The parents stayed behind, waiting to see what was going to happen in Cuba. They did not want to lose all that they had worked for. I am not sure Carmen's parents ever left Cuba.

I planned my future while attending sixth grade—what I was to study and where I wanted to work. Even though the Revolution had started, I thought we would stay in Cuba and somehow things would be normal again. I planned to major in Philosophy and Letters at the University of Havana to become a professor. My idea was to live in Havana during the week and to spend the weekends and vacations in Varadero or another beach. I had been learning English as a second language since first grade and thought that later I would also learn French. My history teacher, a well-dressed, thin and petite brunette with fair skin and dark eyes, mentioned to us in class that she was studying French at the Alliance Française in Havana. She had a degree in Philosophy and Letters. I thought I wanted to do the same. She became my role model. I remember her black leather belt decorated with pins representing different country flags. This was something fashionable at the time, and I copied it as soon as I could. One day, our teacher shared with us that she was soon to be married; her announcement brought a round of applause from the class. It was nice to have a lay teacher for a change. I never saw this teacher after the rebels took over our school, but I assume that she left Cuba, too.

EIGHT

CUBA STARTS TO CHANGE

We returned from Nieves's restaurant at the corner of our house. It was December 31, 1958, around 9:00 p.m. A feeling of uncertainty surrounded us. Everyone seemed uneasy at home. We went downstairs to talk to our neighbor, María Antonia, who was on the sidewalk with her son. My little sister came along. María Antonia worked as the assistant of Lilia Fernández, who headed Cuba's Children and Family Social Services Department, as well as an asylum for the elderly that she created; she also was the sister of Cuba's First Lady. My mother had worked in that department until 1955, when she left due to a difficult second pregnancy. We greeted María Antonia, who leaned over to whisper: "the Man (meaning Batista) is leaving tonight. Fidel will be in control tomorrow. Juan, call your brother and tell him to be careful and to come to Havana and hide. I hear the 'bearded ones' are communists. It's over."

We were surprised by the news but believed and trusted María Antonia. That night we heard many planes flying over Havana, confirming her news and our fears. Early the next day, my father called his brother, who was the mayor of Colón, the town in the Matanzas province where they grew up, to tell him the news. Uncle, who was still incredulous, came to Havana at my father's insistence. Uncle thought everything would be fine even though the regime was changing. A few weeks later, he learned otherwise. He was apprehended by the rebels but quickly released by a general who knew him. My uncle, who was a doctor, had saved the life of the general's brother. After hiding for a month, uncle left Cuba through an embassy with the help of my father. The general, who opposed the extreme measures of Castro's government, was executed.

We always went to church on New Year's Day. January 1, 1959, was different; Batista had left the night before. We went to our neighborhood's church, The Tumbling Down. The church had high ceilings with one altar in the middle and smaller ones on the sides. Paintings of the Stations of the Cross hung on pillars leading to the main altar. The main door always remained open, allowing the sun's rays to illuminate the church. That day, we walked down the main aisle, but turned to sit on a side bench, as if to hide in the crowded church.

Mass started amid a tense mood due to the events of the day. We all knew life was changing, but tried to keep our routines to remain calm. My aunt was nervous. Her husband had a job at the Cuban Electrical Company, partly managed and owned by the U.S. He knew many Batista supporters and had close ties to high ranks of the previous government. She was concerned for her husband's fate and position. When Mass started, a young man with a long beard, dressed in the olive green fatigues of the Revolutionary Army, rushed into church. At first we were scared; we thought he could have a gun or that other rebels could come in to interfere with Mass. People stared. I could tell everyone was uneasy but would not move. We had heard that the Rebels did not like the church. We looked carefully at him. I shuddered, trying to see if he had a gun. "He doesn't have a gun. It's fine. Maybe he's religious," I said. He threw himself on the floor, in the middle of the main aisle facing the altar. He bent on his knees and started rocking front to back, almost in a gesture of someone demented. He proceeded to thank God at the top of his lungs. "Thank you God for freeing us, thank you God for the Revolution! Finally we've won," he shouted. My mother and aunt looked at each other in disbelief that this was happening in our church while Mass was being said. My aunt quickly rose from the bench asking us to leave before the situation got out of control. We got up, walked by the side aisle, avoided eye contact with the rebel and left. We did not stop until we were far from the church. "Marietta, this is not a good omen," said my aunt. She would be proven right.

Havana was under a state of euphoria, even though Fidel Castro had yet to arrive. There were great expectations. The rebels and Castro took one week traveling the Island through main roads, stopping in every major town to rejoice in the triumph of the Revolution, before reaching Havana. Some people said they took time to avoid Batista's men. People were tired of the terror created by those who opposed Batista. Many were upset with Batista for his coup d'état years before, unsatisfied by the involvement of the mafia in gambling casinos, and frustrated by the violation of the Cuban Constitution. Batista, however, was popular before. He created social reforms to help the poor and built roads, schools, and hospitals. Still, the country was not happy with his coup d'état. People listened to some media that promoted Castro. Even the Church and many wealthy families supported Castro, never thinking that later, he would turn against them. Previously, bombs exploded in restaurants and movie theatres to create terror and harm the economy. Once Batista left, the bomb explosions stopped, bringing a feeling of relief. Before, Batista's secret police had tortured some opponents. It was over. The story everyone seemed to believe was that the Revolutionary Army was full of brave young and idealistic fighters who were going to help Cuba get rid of corruption, restore the constitution, and hold elections. However, some people wondered if the rebels were brave since rumors said that Batista's army did not fight towards the end, offering little resistance. Were the rebels so brave and responsible for Cuba's liberation, or was the resistance by citizens in the cities responsible for the changes that eventually took place? The darkest rumors had to do with the beliefs and intentions of the Revolutionary Army. People said many of them were Communists or allied to Cuba's Communist party that intended to change Cuba, not toward a constitutional democracy, but toward a totalitarian state.

Yet, everyone seemed happy, expecting Fidel to arrive in Havana. Finally, when Fidel arrived in the capital, my family decided to stay home and watch his entrance into the city and his speech on television. We disliked crowds, preferring public places that were organized and controlled. It was probably not safe anyway to go and see Fidel in person. It was safer to watch him on the TV screen.

The first speech Fidel gave was attended by what seemed to be at least one hundred thousand people. I was a kid and avidly watched it on TV. It was a nine hour speech. As I listened and watched Fidel with his entourage, who were to save Cuba, I wondered why someone needed so much time to say something, meaningful or not. It seemed to me that his speech was redundant and full of rambling thoughts. I could not remember much of anything he said, which in my young opinion, was a bad sign. I watched his gestures closely and wondered if that was what leaders and revolutionaries looked like. Fidel was boring after awhile. He seemed conceited and mad at everyone except himself. At one point in this speech, a white dove landed on his shoulder and relieved itself. This was supposed to be a sign of good luck, but years later, as the opposition to Fidel grew, the joke was that the white dove knew his intentions before everyone else. Still, even his rambling and long speeches did not discourage many who continued to follow him, believing that he was a genius, worthy of adoration like a god. Everyone had to listen to his tirades. Even some of my relatives liked him, and many in my family had supported Batista. The only person who never liked him was my father, who had not approved of Batista, either. Father remembered Fidel from the University of Havana. "Fidel is nothing better than a gangster. He'll be bad for Cuba," he used to say.

Fidel constantly addressed the country in rallies that were televised to the entire nation. His message, filled with anger and hate, was always derogatory of Cubans who opposed him and of Americans. On the speaking platform he had his closest commanders, Ernesto "Che" Guevara, Camilo Cienfuegos, and a few others who ended up in jail or disappeared. Raúl Castro was there, but never too visible except when he appeared with his wife, Vilma Espín, a woman from a wealthy family that he wed while they were rebels. Another key figure was a woman named Celia Sánchez, a close confidante of Fidel. At a point there were rumors of a romance between the two. As a child, I wondered if that was true. It sounded possible, although she was a tough woman and not particularly attractive. The young rebels were all full of energy, and many of the men were attractive although unkept, but after all, they had been fighting in the mountains; they symbolized an idealistic image for a romantic cause. Camilo was compared to Jesus Christ because of his looks. My family thought this comparison bordered on sacrilege. He was extremely popular, and so was Che Guevara. Camilo was so popular that many Cubans preferred him to Fidel. During the first year of the revolution, Camilo disappeared, never to be found. His helicopter was lost in a flight. No one ever knew what happened. All those who worked in the air control tower in touch with his flight also disappeared, including the nephew of my uncle Estrada. There were rumors that Fidel had Camilo killed, in fear of his popularity. It seemed that Cubans no longer cared about policies or the constitution. They were all following personalities like as one would follow a popularity contest.

Che Guevara was popular too, not as much as Camilo, but he had his following. He talked often on TV after he became the Minister of Economy. One day, as he was speaking on TV, I was watching him with my father; by this time my mother had stopped watching them. Mother knew what they were like and was starting to figure out a future outside of Cuba. I asked dad about Che's speech and economic theories. "Now I am convinced that Cuba's economic future is in trouble. This man is a cretin," commented my father.

Years later Guevara disappeared from Cuba. Cubans were told that he had done his work in Cuba and was going to help bring revolution to

Bolivia. Well, he was immediately killed in Bolivia and subsequently made a hero by Fidel. However, while we were in Cuba, Camilo was never mentioned again. Everyone felt that the Revolution was reluctant to make him a hero. He just died so young, in his twenties. Eventually Fidel would get rid of all who could be competitors.

As the Revolution continued its relentless pace, new faces appeared in Cuba. We asked ourselves, "Who are they?" Then we realized they were Russians or Eastern Europeans! Soon after Fidel took power, we started to see foreigners who did not look like Americans. They were blonder than the Americans we used to see in Havana, not graceful, poorly dressed, and did not speak English or Spanish; they were not buying anything, either. Yes, they were Russians, and we were in amazement. We did not like those foreigners; we preferred the Americans. The Russians boarded our buses and we impolitely stared at them. I think they felt like intruders, but they seemed to like our island. They had old clothes and shoes; they wore summer clothes that no Cuban would wear to go out; their shoes were sandals made out of thick, coarse leather. We never saw that style of sandal anywhere before. We thought, "What is happening to our country? Are they supposed to help us? They look like we could help them, even with our shortages." We all agreed. That was not a good sign. Just like the dove that relieved itself on Fidel.

As the Revolution took over more facets of our lives, a new concept, modeled after Russia, started to appear, the Young Pioneers. These were the elementary school children now attending the government-run schools. They all had to dress the same way and wear a red scarf around their necks, symbolizing the Communist Revolution. They were being trained on all subjects while being indoctrinated on the dogma of the Cuban Revolution. They were being brainwashed early on so that they could have total allegiance to Castro and the Revolution. Gone were the teachings that we knew of Cuban history and heroes. The nation was systematically being erased, its history replaced with new ideas and newly created heroes. That was what my mother had feared, that the regime would take away everything, including the children. Children were being taught by the government who was instilling in them communist values to replace the Christian values and ideas. The goal was to eliminate any loyalty to family and God. Our freedoms were disappearing.

The resistance of the Catholic Youth took place during the early period of the Revolution. Confusion abounded, yet people were still euphoric. Castro started by creating a government with a president. He had to fool the Cuban politicians and wealthy owners who had provided him support with the hope that the Cuban Constitution would be restored and other parties given a voice again. Castro spoke often with speeches that intended to brainwash the masses and to create division among Cuban social classes. He instigated hatred against everything, every institution, and everyone who could be a challenge to him. He started to systematically erase the past. As time passed, everyone wondered, weighed his comments, and became disillusioned. This began to happen to each sector of the population, starting with the most educated and wealthy, until it reached the less fortunate. Castro destroyed between 10 to 20 percent of the population to gain complete control of the remaining 80 percent; still, some of us had hope. There had to be a way to influence Castro; there had to be a way to protest peacefully and to convey a point. That was our hope.

The Catholic Youth held public acts of protest to communicate that religion, the right to be free, and to have choices mattered. Many of those acts took place in Havana. Many of us placed stickers on walls to protest. We were full of youthful illusions. While we were exercising our right to protest, hoping to make a change, more schools were taken over, more people were sent to gallows and killed without trials at the firing squads, a concept instituted by Ernesto "Che" Guevara.

As days and months went by, more things continued to change rapidly. First, anyone who was involved with the previous regime was persecuted, killed by the firing squads, or thrown in jail. As a child I was struck by this terror and became afraid. *Bohemia*, a popular magazine, published photos of civilians who had been tortured by Batista's regime. Then they published photos of Batista's men killed by Castro's firing squads. It seemed to me there was no difference. Eventually *Bohemia*, as all other media, was controlled by the Revolution. The media had to publish only what was approved by the government. Only positive commentary was welcomed and allowed. Everyone who dissented was against Cuba and unpatriotic.

At first the government had a president. Then Fidel decided to be in full control. "Have elections for what purpose? We do not need elections," he said in one of his speeches. Nobody challenged him for fear of dying. First was the agrarian reform that took land from owners. The land became the property of the government. Then all businesses were nationalized without compensation. The currency changed, and people were forced to exchange the old money for the new in a matter of days, losing what could not be exchanged. Personal accounts were seized. Guns were taken away from the people so that they could not defend themselves. Nuns and priests were forced to leave the country while the government took over all the Catholic or religious schools. Then the urban reform was instituted, taking private property away from owners. Next, the government decided to create the revolutionary committees to spy on all its citizens. Each street block had a committee watching and reporting to the government what private citizens did; they had to watch for counter-revolutionary acts to protect the Revolution. Later, the government promoted community and volunteer work. Everyone had to participate in name of the Revolution. People started to disappear from sight. They were either killed or sent to concentration camps.

We heard there was going to be an invasion by Cubans who opposed the Revolution, backed by the United States. This was the last hope for all of those who had realized that change meant communism. We anxiously waited, and much to our frustration, we heard the news that the Revolutionary government had defeated the invasion. People said the young Cuban fighters were holding up well but were waiting for air support from the United States that never came. They were defeated in seventy-two hours, and all ended up in jail. Castro took this opportunity to cement the communist Revolution. He televised the trial where each of the invaders was questioned and humiliated. There was a black fighter whom he addressed personally, asking him, "And what are you doing in this invasion? You, of all people, should be with the Revolution." The fighter answered that his skin color did not have anything to do with his beliefs. Castro moved on to interview another fighter. I watched the trials for hours. My parents confirmed their belief at that point that we definitely needed to leave the country, while there was still time.

It all happened quickly, in frenzy. No one had time to react or to fight back. Confusion and fear reigned. No one could be trusted. People started to leave during the first two years of the Revolution and have continued to leave ever since. Our family decided to take a risk and leave. Staying meant losing our freedom; leaving meant finding it. We were convinced that following a madman and remaining in a country without a constitution and laws could only bring us bad consequences.

NINE

GETTING READY TO LEAVE

While my parents planned the necessary steps to leave Cuba, they explained them to me. I remember the discussions in my house when the subject came up: should we stay or leave? We saw how quickly things were changing in Cuba. The turn of events left no doubt that the new regime was not restoring the Constitution. The government's cabinet seemed to be a puppet one. The rebels were executing those who had worked with the Batista regime and incarcerating citizens for their religious beliefs, for who they were, or for false accusations of counter-revolutionary activities. Established institutions that opposed the Revolution were dissolved. The gains that the country had made prior to the Revolution in medicine, social services, women's rights, education, and union rights were ignored. People were told that the country's 90 percent literacy rate and the many roads, schools, and hospitals built by Batista were created by the Revolution. The new government intervened in private and religious schools, took property away from owners, froze bank accounts, and changed the currency. A feeling of terror started to spread through the island. Rumors were rampant. Everyone was touched and affected as the Revolution persecuted and destroyed layer upon layer of the society. The new leaders created a divisive feeling between social classes and animosity against the United States. Mothers were afraid that their children would be taken from them and sent to schools to be indoctrinated. Mother told my father: "We're leaving. Look at what's happening here. This Revolution is destroying our society with false excuses. They can take our property and jobs, but not our children." Father agreed but was concerned about his ability to make a living abroad. He was the general manager of a Cuban design and manufacturing firm that built and installed professional kitchens in hotels, restaurants, and hospitals. When the business was intervened in, father resigned from his job to leave Cuba. Somehow, he thought that things would change and he would be able to work again. Mother reasoned with him saying, "The unknown has got to be better than the known taking place here!"

Mother went to see Havana's Catholic archbishop, a friend of her family, to discuss her decision. We went with Aunt María, father's sister. We waited inside the church while mother met with the archbishop in his office. I sat on a bench, looking around the large and empty church. People were not going to church anymore, afraid of being singled as religious and persecuted by the government. I confided to my aunt that I was concerned about mother's decision. I loved Cuba, my life, and my family and did not want to leave. "Don't worry. Your mother is doing this because she wants the best for all of you. We're not leaving, and we'll be here to receive you when you return. This will pass. Cubans won't support a communist regime. In two years you'll be back," she said. I saw the light piercing through the church's open door and looked at the altar. "Are you sure?" I asked. "Yes, in two years," she said. I thought it was going to take longer but kept quiet. I never saw my aunt again.

We had to get passports, among other things. We had our pictures taken and requested the papers. The most difficult part was to inform the government that we were planning to leave. We had to explain ourselves to them. We got the pictures, and we did not like them, but they had to do. We completed the forms and presented them to the government, hoping everything would go smoothly. I remember going to the government's office in Old Havana, near El Malecón and the Old Fortress and thinking what a nice day it was but how awful it was to have to lie to the government officials during our interview. I already felt like an outcast in my own country. This new feeling was unwelcomed by me. We still had to obtain visas. That was complicated, for they had to come from the United States, requested by a contact overseas and granted by the U.S. government. Two of our relatives were already in the United States with their families: one was my father's brother and the other, Joaquin, my mother's cousin. They were claiming the four of us. I requested a student visa to enter the U.S. Once in the United States, I was to claim political asylum. The last document we needed was a plane ticket to travel from Cuba to the United States. Those tickets could not be purchased in Cuba; they had to be sent to you by an overseas relative or friend. We then had to wait for the Cuban government to process our request and to give a permit with a date to leave.

Once my family decided to leave Cuba, my mother wanted me to improve my English. I had never worried too much about mastering English, although I took my homework seriously and always got good grades. My father already knew the language. My uncle Lázaro, my father's other brother, spoke English well; he learned it taking courses in the public schools. There were academies that taught mostly business and English courses to older kids and adults. Ironically, Uncle Lázaro was the one who never left Cuba. He could not decide early enough what to do. After 1962, he was not allowed to leave. He was an orthopedic surgeon, and the government could not afford to lose any more doctors. I signed up for classes, thinking I would attend as long as I could. At this point, I no longer went to my private Catholic school; the government had taken it over. Everything in our lives was in transition, just like the country. It seemed that we were also in a holding pattern, waiting for the approval to go on with our lives. Our past had disappeared; almost nothing was as we knew it. Our present required constant adaptability and improvisation as well as alertness to protect ourselves. Our future was unknown and dangerous. Everyday tasks were a way to keep some sanity and stability. I submerged myself in this new activity of improving my language skills. I had never attended a public school, but once I was there, I liked it. Our class was made up of teenagers and young adults. Although I was twelve, I looked older since I was tall for my age. I thought I looked at least fourteen. I kept thinking of my uncle and how he learned English in a similar school; it gave me hope that I could speak better someday. I hoped for it with all my heart. The classes made me practice what I already knew and provided the training of wondering about an unknown social setting, an adjustment that would require more effort than merely learning a language. This type of adaptation would come in handy in the future.

Just after the government started to take over the private Catholic schools, they started persecuting the religious orders. There were many private schools in Cuba run by different religious denominations: the Teresian School and the Ursulinas taught classes in Spanish; the French Dominicans, in French; and the Mercy School, in English. They were all-girl schools. Boys had their own private schools, such as Belén and La Salle. La Progresiva was a co-ed Protestant private school. My uncle Lázaro's daughters went to La Progresiva since his wife was Presbyterian and her church ran the school. The Revolution's armed militiamen and women supervised the religious orders during class and communicated with their presence that the schools now belonged to the government. As weeks progressed, the nuns had to leave the schools and move to convents or their family homes. Carmen Susana, my mother's cousin, moved to her mother's house. She no longer wore a religious habit. Her hair was short. She was worried and scared, waiting for instructions from her religious order, the Carmelites, as to what her future would be. Some priests and nuns had already been taken prisoners. There were rumors that some were being killed. No one knew what their fate would be.

We knew Carmen Susana would leave Cuba soon. She had been my first grade teacher who taught me to read and write. We spent a night at her mother's house to say good-bye. I slept in her bed. She wore a white cotton gown, looking like any one of us. She became another person without her habit. It struck me. I always thought of nuns as beings from another world, closer to Heaven than to Earth. We spoke about what this change meant to her. She was spiritual and encouraged me to have faith while facing adversity. She explained that faith was needed the most in moments like the ones we were living in. She offered me a scholarship at a Carmelite school to continue my studies abroad without interruption. She gave us three options: Spain, Venezuela, or the United States. My parents chose the United States since they were going to Miami. My future was settled. That night was the last time that we saw each other.

Jorge Luis, the son of Jorge, another of my mother's cousins, was taken as political prisoner by Castro. Everyone wondered what would happen to him. Luckily, the charges against him were dropped. Jorge and his wife left Cuba for Puerto Rico with their three daughters and son.

The news arrived in October 1961. I was given a date to leave the country alone. The four of us could not leave together as we wished. I told my mother that I would not leave alone. She disagreed. I argued, "What if you can't leave? I may never see you again. I won't go." I was angry at the government for separating us, sad, and scared. My life was out of my control. I had to trust in God. Mother said, "You're free to do what you want but think of this: we'll leave sooner or later and you'll have lost your visa and your chance to leave. When we're notified, we'll leave you behind. You won't be able to leave with us." I offered to stay with my relatives who were not planning to leave. "When they give me another permit later, I'll join you," I said. "You can do that. It's your decision. If I were you, I'd leave. Think about it tonight and decide. You have until tomorrow to tell me what you'll do," said mother. I turned the thought over and over in my head that night, reaching the conclusion that staying meant losing the opportunity to leave. If my family was not allowed out of Cuba, I could always return. I had to go.

Throughout this whole period of uncertainty, the image of my parents remained strong in my memory. My mother became the leader who took care of all the steps to leave. She assessed the unfolding situation, researched options, talked with friends and family, and laid out a plan that she kept discussing with my father. My mother had no doubt that we had to leave Cuba, but my father did. Her concern was with the safety and future of her two daughters. She did not want our family to live under a communist government. My father wanted to protect us but was concerned with the unknown and the ability to earn a living outside of Cuba for all of us. My father's family was divided: some were leaving, although in their minds only temporarily, while others were staying to wait and see what happened. He had two brothers and two sisters. One brother, the ex-mayor of Colón, had already left, the other brother, Lázaro, was staying waiting for things to change, to somehow correct themselves. One sister was leaving and the other, Aunt María, was staying; she and her husband could not believe that a communist regime could dominate Cuba. My father was concerned with what awaited him in a new country, but he did not support the Revolution. My mother's family was leaving. Her cousin Luis, his mother and aunts, as well as Cuca and Antón already had processed the papers to leave and were waiting the approval from the government. My mother believed that we were facing the unknown anyway and that the United States and political exile was the unknown with a promise of freedom. Cuba was becoming the known with the certain promise of jail.

When the day came for me to leave, I got ready. The government allowed you to take a ninety-pound bag. People were making light long sacks with zippers to put in their belongings. I took some clothes and wore a new red and white dress with a wide brown leather belt and brown low heel shoes with a matching purse. I wore small gold-plated hoop earrings that I still own and that I had purchased at Woolworth or Tencen, as we used to call the store. By the time I left, I had just turned thirteen but dressed to look older. I could not take good jewelry or any other possessions, just a few pesos (equivalent at that time to the U.S. dollar) and some family photographs.

My relatives came to see me off. We sat in a glass room called the fishbowl, waiting my turn to go. When they called my name, I kissed them goodbye. I went through an inspection line. "Why are you leaving Cuba?" asked the guard. "To study," I answered. "Will you return?" he asked. "Yes," I answered. They instructed me to walk outside. I turned to my relatives and sadly waved goodbye. It was a beautiful sunny day. I climbed the stairs to board the plane and sat two rows behind the pilot. Other children, younger than me, were leaving alone too. I glanced at the horizon and the palm trees around the airport, realizing that I might never see my country or my parents and relatives again. I was going to be cut off from my roots. "When will I come back?" I asked myself. A voice, not my own, answered me, "Never before forty years." "But that's a lifetime," I answered in my head. "Yes, it'll be a lifetime before you're able to return." I never returned.

TEN

IN THE U.S.A.

I arrived in Miami on October 18, 1961, on a Havana-Miami Pan Am flight. Joaquín, one of my mother's cousins, met me. He took me to stay with his family while the U.S. Immigration Department processed my papers, and I was able to go to my final destination, St. Teresa's Academy in Texas.

Even though Havana was a city with more than a million inhabitants, I thought that the city was not large—and it really was not—compared to other places. I envisioned cities in the U.S. to be big, just like the country and to have dark, brick buildings with different vegetation from ours. This idea quickly disappeared from my head as I found to my amazement that Miami had the same warm sun and even more humidity than Cuba. Miami seemed to me to be more like a town that you would find in the interior of Cuba. At that time, it did not have the look of a city the way Havana did. The houses and restaurants looked to me like doll houses, which was disappointing. "Is this how the U.S. looks? But Havana is such a big, sophisticated city next to Miami! Well, I will have to get used to it. God only knows how many other surprises I will have," I thought.

Joaquin and his wife had a son and daughter who were not close to me. Joaquin, like his brother Luis, was a society column journalist. He had worked for *Avance,* one of Havana's better-known newspapers, and his wife had been a wealthy socialite. They had been well-off in Havana, but now they lived in a tiny apartment. She had to take care of the household and work to earn money. The situation was a little chaotic for her. Joaquín had to intervene in her attempts to discipline their kids because they only listened to him. When I stayed with them, we ate at small coffee shops and bought TV dinners to eat at home. I remember dining out with them and the fights that Carmita, Joaquín's wife, had with her rebellious nine-year old daughter to get her to eat her meals. Her fourteen-year old son looked upon them with indifference, as if he were above it all. The kids were both beautiful and nice to me. Joaquín and his wife went out of their way to make me feel welcome and protected. I appreciated that they shared their food and apartment with me. Joaquín had already bought a used car and took me to all the meetings with Immigration. Those steps were a little scary for me, but I found the U.S. government officials nice and helpful, with a serious but non-threatening attitude, unlike those in Cuba. Finally, I got clearance after a few days to stay in the country as a political refugee. I could now go to San Antonio as planned to wait for my parents while I studied.

The day I left for San Antonio I was unusually nervous. I knew that with that step I would be totally cut off from my family and wondered how things would go. I had studied English in Cuba, understood the grammar rules, and could read but did not speak or understand a word people said to me. In San Antonio I was to meet a religious sister from the Teresian School. I was to become a boarder, something I always wanted to experience, while waiting for my parents and sister to arrive in the United States. Then I would join them in Miami where we planned to live.

I did not know the sister who was to greet me and pick me up, but figured that she would be wearing the same religious habit they wore in Cuba. I hoped that she would be friendly and would speak Spanish. I also hoped to get on the right flight and to be able to get off where I was supposed to go since I had to change planes. On the way to San Antonio I got so nervous that I threw up as we landed. The people sitting next to me looked at me in disgust. I thought that they would not have been so upset if they knew what I was going through. Probably, had I been in their place, I would have been disgusted too. The flight attendant came to my rescue. I explained, in my broken English, that I had come from Cuba a couple of weeks ago, I was alone and nervous, I was to meet someone, and I was scared of getting lost. She was nice and understanding and told me not to worry. "I will take care of cleaning this. These things happen, and good luck to you," she said while I tried to clean up. I was relieved.

Finally, I found myself at the crowded San Antonio airport with no idea where to go. I quickly searched for the familiar religious habit and to my relief, found it right away. There she was, with a big smile, wearing a white habit instead of the brown one that nuns wore in Cuba. I walked towards her to introduce myself in English but she responded in Spanish. "I'm Sister Trinidad. I'm also Cuban. Welcome to San Antonio. Let's get your bag and go to your new home. Eight other Cuban girls will be your family. They're staying with us while they wait for their parents," she said. I had overcome another hurdle of many more to come in this new stage of my life. As we drove to the school and saw the brick building, I thought, "This city looks like the United States should."

I stayed eight months at St. Teresa's Academy. We were fourteen boarders, nine from Cuba, and five from Nicaragua, Mexico, Panama, and the United States. Two other Cuban girls who attended classes lived with their family, who settled in San Antonio after leaving Cuba. The idea of living in a boarding school had intrigued me, but I did not envision it this way, without ready access to my parents and not knowing if I would ever see them again. A quick adjustment was necessary.

Life was strict, comfortable, and sometimes fun at St. Teresa's Academy. The nuns took good care of us. Because we were political exiles running away from communism, various charitable organizations helped us. One lady who lost her only, young daughter to cancer invited us for lunch on a Saturday. She opened a closet for us to try her daughter's clothes on and take what we wanted. She watched us picking dresses. I joyfully tried things on but felt embarrassed. What could she be feeling, I thought? But the lady was happy that we were thrilled. She stayed in my mind as a warm and generous woman. Could I have done the same, I wondered? The dress that I picked became a favorite of mine that I wore for many years.

All the boarders got along well. The Cuban girls stuck together. We laughed and cried together and told each other about our families, our sorrows, and our hopes. The Cuban group consisted of girls between nine and eighteen years of age who had lived in different provinces of Cuba and attended the Teresian School in their respective cities. All of us, with the exception of the daughter of a Cuban tobacco company owner, Trinidad y Hnos, were in the San Antonio school under a special scholarship developed for the unique situation in which we found ourselves. All Cuban girls formed a special bond that lasted while we were boarders and, in some cases, for a few years after this experience. The other boarders, the regular ones, as we called them, who came from Mexico, Nicaragua, Panama, and the United States, were not part of our clique. The girls from Latin America were in school to learn English, but I was never quite certain why one of the

American girls lived in the school, for she never shared the reason with us. I remember someone saying that her mother had died and her father traveled.

I remember our Cuban boarders: Milagros was about sixteen, tall, on the heavy side, with dark curly hair and hazel eyes. She was the daughter of a cigar plantation owner. She made it clear to all of us that while we were there under a special scholarship, she was paying her way. We did not appreciate her tone. Like all of us, she found herself powerless, at the mercy of others and facing an unknown future. Isabelita was sixteen, with a petite and slim frame, curly blondish hair, vivid black eyes, and freckles. She had a sweet disposition and was friendly and artistic. She was our guitar player and singer during our moments of leisure. Ana María was seventeen, not too tall, with dark soft hair, big hazel eyes, and a serious and mature attitude. She finished high school at the end of our school year and got engaged towards the end of summer to handsome Ignacio, who was from a wealthy Cuban family. The Arango twins were twelve-years old. They had light golden-brown curly hair and big pale green eyes. Both were thin and tall with a quiet, friendly and well-mannered demeanor. Like so many others, they were from the Camagüey province, and in their case, from an aristocratic family. Then there was Carola, the emotional one. She was sixteen and had blondish-brown hair and hazel-greenish eyes. Her complexion was without blemishes. Her expressive hands, with perfectly shaped nails, made a point while she talked and gestured. The Matas girl was the youngest in our group, just nine years old. She was thin and brunette, with big brown sad eyes. She kept mostly to herself, although she would not shut herself completely from us. In her eyes one could see her concern and confusion. Her father, once a powerful commander of Castro's army, had just been sentenced to twenty years in a political prison for disagreeing with Fidel when he declared himself a Marxist-Leninist and Cuba a Socialist Republic. Sandy was fifteen years old, on the short side with blond hair and brown eyes. She was the rebel in the group. I was thirteen years old, of medium to tall height, thin, with black silky hair and big brown eyes.

All of us stuck together once we were thrown into this situation by a Revolution that we hardly understood. It was a Revolution that hit us hard, turning our lives upside down, tearing us from our roots, country, families, and from everything that we knew and protected us. We became sisters supporting each other when one was depressed. We wrote to our families every week and anxiously waited for their letters.

We followed the daily news about Cuba. Finally, mother called me from Miami to say she and my sister had arrived, but that father was held back in Cuba. My heart pounded fast as I heard the news. I was happy to know my mother and sister were safe but worried for my father. What would we do if he could not leave? Many times before my mother arrived in the U.S., I played different scenarios in my head of how I would survive if my parents could not leave Cuba. Luckily, eleven days later, father arrived in Florida.

Boarding school expanded my knowledge of food. I learned about doughnuts, which became a favorite snack, especially if they were glazed. They just seemed to be made of air and disappeared in your mouth as soon as you bit into them. Potato chips, sweet potatoes, and Mexican food were a novelty. None of the Cuban girls liked sweet potatoes, and we had to figure out how to get rid of them without the nun who supervised our cafeteria noticing. We found out that the legs of our tables were hollow, providing a place where we could stuff the sweets potatoes. The stench of stale food stuck in the table's legs eventually could be smelled in the dining room, forcing us to figure out a new way to eliminate the hated item from our plates. We rotated tables to sit by the window. We dispensed with the sweet potatoes through the open window when the supervising nun was not looking our way. One day, while we walked outdoors, we passed by the side of the building where the cafeteria was located. The nun who accompanied us noticed all the napkins that were accumulated on the ground below the window sill. We acted innocently and continued walking past the mounds of dumped napkins with sweet potatoes inside.

On certain days of the week, we helped Sister Trinidad, the nun in charge of all the Cuban boarders, to clean the floors of our classrooms. She taught us how to use a mop and the bucket to squeeze the mop. What a contraption! In Cuba, our maids only had to use a stick in the form of a "T" with a piece of cloth thrown over it to clean our floors. We became experts at mopping floors. The working sessions with Sister Trinidad allowed us to get closer to her by asking questions or sharing our concerns. While we mopped the floors, we were able to communicate with her in an informal way. One day, as we were finishing our chores, Sister Trinidad asked me if I or any of the other girls had a religious vocation. I quickly said no, but then felt sad for my answer. Surely Sister Trinidad wanted to hear a "yes." I was wrong. She laughed, and, with her usual practicality and good sense of humor, looked at me and said, "Then I must introduce you and the others to some Cuban boys so that you can start dating and eventually form families." I agreed with this idea. Although I was still too young to date, some other boarders were not.

We learned to make our beds, turn our mattresses to air them, iron our uniforms, clean our rooms, and stand in line while a nun checked us to see if were up to their standard before we could go to Mass and classes. This was the routine to be strictly followed Monday through Friday unless we wanted to repeat a chore, with no extra time, and be ready by 6:30 a.m. Going to daily Mass was more than I wished for, but there was not another option. After getting ready for the day, we went to the school's chapel. Our Saturdays started late, at 8 a.m. There was no rush to get ready. Our beds were left to air as we put on our uniforms without ties and enjoyed a leisurely breakfast. Later in the morning, we went up to our dormitories to shower and make our beds. There were no inspection lineups. We enjoyed the rest of the day as we pleased. The only scheduled items were lunch and dinner. We used the study rooms to read or play. A big room was our playground where ping pong or table tennis games went on for hours. We were very competitive with each other's teams and determined to win. Our afternoons were spent in the school yard where some of us played the guitar and sang the Cuban songs that we remembered. We ran around and talked and gossiped. Sandy, the Cuban boarder who had a discipline problem, had the tendency to jump over the wall surrounding our yard on weekends. She would go out, and no one knew where to. The nuns were always worried about her safety, but she always came back and then got scolded. We thought that she had found a boyfriend but never confirmed it. Our after dinner evenings were spent in another room where we played, listened to music, and danced. I had never danced with a girl before, but there were no boys in school, so we practiced our dancing steps with each other.

Sunday was our day to go out. The nuns took us in excursions to various places in San Antonio. We visited the River Walk and went to the movies in the downtown section. One movie theatre intrigued me because of its amazing ceiling painted in blue with many stars, just like the sky. We went to El Alamo, a visit that taught me more about the country's history. We were allowed to go out with families who were from San Antonio and belonged to charitable organizations that were helping us. Each Cuban girl was adopted by a family who took us to lunches and made us feel welcome and loved. My adopting family was Mexican-American with roots in San Antonio for several generations. They invited me to their large Spanish colonial house and gave parties in my honor. When the lady of the house learned that I was leaving San Antonio to join my parents, who had arrived in the United States, she threw a huge party for me. I remember her being tall and thin with dark hair and eyes, elegant and warm. I still envision her coming down the swirling staircase toward the large patio where we were gathered. She gave me a present to help me remember her family, a gesture that I was not expecting. The gift, a leather jewelry box with a pair of Spanish enameled earrings and brooch with pearls, is still in my possession. I was awed and started crying. Sadly, I thought as I looked at the gift, that I probably would not have much occasion to wear the earrings and brooch. I had no clothes, no events to attend, but then I remembered the black dress that the other American lady had given me. I thought that it would look good with the jewelry. I kept the dress and jewelry so that I could wear them once I was reunited with my parents and was a little older.

During the school year I befriended two Cuban girls from Camagüey who were sisters and whose family already lived in San Antonio. When summer came around, all the boarders left school except for Ana María and me. All the other Cuban girls already had their families to go to. The Latin American girls went home to return the following year. One of the American girls stayed in school and went out with her father when he was available. The other American girl went back to Corpus Christi to return the following year. She always talked about how beautiful the beaches were in her home town and, in my mind, I envisioned them to be like Varadero Beach. I had nowhere to go even though my parents were in the United States because they did not know where they would end up living. They were looking for jobs in Miami or hoping to be relocated to another city by the U.S. government. The idea of staying alone in school depressed me. Then the Cuban family of my two school friends invited me and Ana María to stay with them. I cried with joy. I moved into their small but loving home and became another daughter during one month. I wore the few clothes that were gifts instead of the uniform, and while I helped around the house, I did not have inspection every morning. I felt independent and self-sufficient thanks to all that I learned in boarding school.

Life with this Cuban family was like being with relatives. They took care of Ana María and me just as if we were daughters. Everyone had to adjust to smaller-than-usual living quarters with jobs that no one had ever done. The two daughters, Tere and Chiqui, never picked up after themselves. It was obvious that they were not in the boarding school. Their mother would pick up the clothes that her daughters left scattered in the bedroom. Tere and Chiqui were not cooperative. One day the mother got tired and told them to pick up after themselves. She used to check their underwear to make sure it was clean. If not, she made them wash it. Tere never wanted to wash her bras. Her mother scolded her saying "What if you are in a car accident? What would people say when they see your dirty bra?" To which Tere would reply that if she was ever in a car accident, who on earth would care about her bra? I gave some credit to her mother for trying, but I guessed Tere was right.

We enjoyed San Antonio during that month. The River Walk stayed in my mind throughout all these years, just as its downtown theatres and my friends did. Ana María and Tere, the oldest daughter of the family who took us in, were dating two Cuban young men who were in the armed forces and stationed in San Antonio. I went out with them, enjoying being escorted by handsome and uniformed men.

One afternoon, Sister Trinidad visited me to tell me I was to leave in a day to join my family in Chicago. I did not expect Chicago. "What happened to the idea of living in Miami?" I asked. "No jobs," she answered. I was happy and nervous at the same time. Mixed emotions overwhelmed me. I asked her on what airline I was leaving. She looked gloomy. I felt something else was going wrong. I had to ride in a Greyhound bus for two days. I almost died. I did not want to ride a bus alone at my age. Sister Trinidad helped me to overcome my fear. She had welcomed me to San Antonio and now was seeing me off. She became my surrogate mother while I was in Texas and helped me to understand the new way of life. Thanks to her, I was not held back one grade when I arrived. She had explained to me that I knew the subject matter at a more advanced level; all I needed was to learn English quickly to move on to that class. The nuns forced us to speak English amongst ourselves. Some days, when we were too tired and missed our families and customs too much, we turned to Spanish in consolation. Whenever we saw a nun, we stopped talking and started to laugh, since laughter was a universal language. One day, standing in line, a nun spoke to us. I could not figure out in what language she had spoken, but I understood what she said. Since she did not speak Spanish, I realized that I had learned English. I moved to the eighth grade. Sister Trinidad was always right. I could trust her.

Once at the Greyhound station, Sister Trinidad kissed me goodbye. A fear overcame me, thinking about spending two days and a night alone on the bus. I had to figure out how to protect myself. I spotted a young woman with a daughter and introduced myself, explaining that I was alone, traveling to Chicago to meet my parents, who had just arrived from Cuba. I asked her if I could hang around with them to make it look that we were together. She agreed. I was relieved. My trip went well. As the bus arrived in Chicago, I prepared myself mentally for the reunion with my parents and sister. I did not know what to expect after all this time. I felt changed and wondered if they had changed, too. I spotted my family waiting for me. We hugged and kissed each other, thanking God to be safe and united again. They thought I was taller and thinner, looking grown up. My parents looked to me thinner, older, and somewhat apprehensive, but happy to be together. My sister was taller; her pretty blondish and curly hair was now long.

We took the subway to our apartment. Chicago, a city that all the boarders in San Antonio told me was full of gangsters, seemed somber and gray. I was happy to be with my family again but all of a sudden felt that I no longer was a young girl in spirit. I had grown up. I was physically close to my parents again, yet far away, an independent being. At that moment I realized that my family life, as I had known it before the Cuban Revolution, had ended. Our neighborhood and acquaintances were lost forever. A new life was unfolding. It was Father's Day, June 1962.

EPILOGUE

Most of my relatives ended up leaving Cuba, opposing Castro, and losing all their possessions. Other relatives remained in Cuba, going through all of its changes and hardships, continuing their lives. My uncle Lázaro and his family stayed. He remained an orthopedic surgeon and the director of Cárdenas Hospital, my aunt retired from being a nurse, his three daughters became medical doctors, and two had to serve the Cuban government in the Angolan war. Lázaro continued to do deep sea fishing in his motor boat. After we were in the United States, we learned that his boat was confiscated by the Castro government. They were afraid that he would leave and they could not afford to lose any more doctors. My Aunt María stayed. She continued to be a teacher while her husband, Estrada, stopped practicing law. Her daughter became a medical doctor.

My mother's old aunts, Pepa, Amita, Cándida and her cousin, Luis, were planning to leave, but when Cuca and Antón became ill, they decided to wait. Luis later ended up in a political prison. My mother's aunts died in Cuba. When we reunited, my father told us that after my mother and sister left Cuba, Cuca and Antón were devastated. Two years later they died. Antón died of cancer and Cuca of a heart attack when she learned that Antón had cancer. She died first. All their illusions had died, too. My parents often spoke of them. My sister always keeps their photograph in her bedroom. I tell my mother how many of my sister's mannerisms, personal tastes, and reactions in life remind me of Cuca, as if her spirit continues to live on.

Carmen Susana, the Carmelite nun who was my mother's cousin, moved to Venezuela and later to Colombia, where she taught grammar school at the Teresian School. We continued to write and call each other throughout the years. After she lived in Colombia, while traveling to Miami to see her brother Joaquín, her airplane was hijacked to Cuba. She thought that she would die, but nothing happened to her. She never flew again. She taught until her death in Bogotá, Colombia.

Joaquín and his family moved to Puerto Rico for a few years and back to Miami, where he was able to write a social column for the newspaper *Diario de las Américas* until he passed away. He also published various editions of the book *Yearly Guide of Cuban Families* that featured all the exiled Cubans and kept families in touch with each other.

Other members of my mother's family ended up scattered among a few countries. Carina and her family moved to Puerto Rico to be with her brother Jorge and his family. Jorge's daughters established businesses in Puerto Rico, and his son Jorge Luis, who was going to play baseball in Cuba, became a baseball scout and in turn, his son, a baseball player with a U.S. major league team. Carina's sons also graduated from the University of Puerto Rico and worked in various enterprises, as did Joaquin's children. Pepito, another of my mother's cousin, who used to manage the funeral home that the family owned in Cuba, moved to New Jersey with his family. Marcelito and Teté, Carmen Luisa, my mother's sister, and her family, Cuca's brother Panchito, his second wife, Nélida, and his daughters Suzi and Conchi, and their mother moved to Miami, as well as other maternal relatives. Carmen Luisa's children grew up and studied in Florida and Tennessee, where her son became a doctor. The sons and daughter of Berta, another beloved cousin of my mother, moved to the United States. All established successful families and careers. One of the sons became a scientist who contributed inventions to the health sciences field.

My paternal uncle, the ex-mayor, revalidated his medical doctor's license and specialized in hematology, oncology, and pathology and became the manager of the pathology and nuclear medicine department of a Chicago hospital until he died. He had a successful career in medicine and conducted much research on the relationship between AIDS and lymphatic cancer. My uncles, who drove me to Varadero Beach, were able to find jobs in their professional fields: my aunt as a teacher and my uncle as an engineer. Their son graduated as an engineer from the University of Illinois and later obtained an MBA. He developed a career in engineering and real estate. My sister also went to the same university, where she obtained a degree in sociology and psychology. Later, she established a successful private practice as an intuitive consultant. My father was able to find work in Chicago. Eventually he became the production department's supervisor of a privately-held company that manufactured commercial sewing machines. He worked there for twenty years until he retired. My mother worked in a small company that sold women's fashions by catalogue until she retired.

Osvaldito's family moved to Puerto Rico where they established an insurance business like the one they owned in Cuba. They often visited Aunt Carmen Luisa once they moved to Miami. We ran into Osvaldito's mother and sister at Miami's Versailles Restaurant, a place where Cubans gather. Carmen, my schoolmate from the Teresian School in Havana, moved to Spain with her brother and sister. We kept in touch for years. She often wrote me how lonely they were. She never talked about her parents. Eventually her brother moved to France to find work to help support the family. Then we lost touch with each other.

I never saw any of my friends from Varadero again. Once we were in our early twenties, one of my male cousins mentioned that he had run into Pupy, whose hands were beaten up because he was working as a fisherman. He stopped his studies to work. It was hard to imagine that because Pupy's family had been so well-off, but it happened all the time to the Cubans who had gone into exile and whose lives took a completely new turn.

One day, also at Versailles Restaurant, I ran into Carola, my schoolmate from St. Teresa's Academy in Texas. She looked the same to me, just more mature; she was with her mother. I kept in touch with Ana María, who invited me to her wedding with Ignacio, but when they decided to cancel the wedding, she stopped writing, and we lost touch with each other. Sister Trinidad and I corresponded with each other until she died. She even visited Chicago at one point and got to meet my parents.

Luis, my mother's cousin, who was a well-known society column journalist, stayed in Cuba after we left, waiting for his permit to leave. He no longer worked in the newspaper *El Diario de la Marina*, the number one paper before Castro, since it had been shut down by the government. Luis had been helping Cubans who were persecuted by Castro to leave through embassies. Those activities landed him in a Castro political prison. I never knew all the details of his apprehension but heard that he was shot and sentenced to thirty years. He was kept in a high security prison in Havana.

Three years after Luis was imprisoned, our family was contacted by Fidel Castro's regime. They said they would release Luis if we paid their government $30,000 dollars in a week. We were ecstatic, but at the same time worried that we could not get the ransom money gathered that quickly; after all, Castro had already taken everything we owned. All of Luis' relatives began a collection campaign to gain his freedom. Everyone we contacted donated whatever they could to buy his freedom. Luis had to leave Cuba immediately after being freed. His mother and aunts already had died; now he felt that he could leave too. Luis and his wife Delia moved to Madrid, Spain just before Francisco Franco died. Luis could have moved to the United States but chose Spain because he did not master the English language. He felt differently than his other journalist brother. How could he work as a journalist if he did not know English? His friends, who owned a retail store chain in Spain, El Corte Inglés, employed him in their public relations department.

My sister and I visited Luis and his wife Delia in Madrid during our first trip to Europe, fourteen years after we left Cuba. He showed us around the city. He and his wife gave a small dinner party for us. We ate in his beautiful apartment, furnished with belongings and antiques from Cuba that he had taken out through an embassy. I remember that he picked us up at a café where we were sitting with a Cuban couple who was in our tour group. When Luis walked in, everyone turned to look at him. He had a strong presence and an elegance that made people notice him. The Cuban couple from our tour could not believe that it was Luis. They told us that he was well known, to which we replied that we knew it because he was our mother's cousin and my godfather. At his apartment we talked about our lives, work, and earnings. He said to me that I earned more than he did. I was embarrassed, but he was not. He was happy for me. Here was a man who was well known, had known every influential person in Havana, and had been wealthy, yet was humble and able to accept his place in life every moment of it. I was proud of him. I asked him about his experience in the political prison. He talked briefly, explaining that he had a bullet in him for three years, suffered of asthma attacks, and was constantly mentally tortured. He told us that the guards made them strip naked at night and took them out to the yard to be shot. Then, the guards returned them to their cells in the darkness. He led his cell making all the men pray daily and read the Bible. Those acts saved the men in his cell and him. I asked him to tell me more, but he said "You do not want to know more." "Would you ever return to Cuba if you could?" I asked. "No. Cubans were not good to me. They repaid me poorly. I will never return." He was right. He had established various charities and helped to found the Cuban Ballet but was not recognized for any of it. He died in Madrid. He never returned to Cuba. Neither have we.

www.ingramcontent.com/pod-product-compliance
Lightning Source LLC
Chambersburg PA
CBHW021234280526
45784CB00005B/2091